Turn To *God* From Idols

*Eternity is a long time,
choose God before it is too late.*

*Live the blessed life now
and through eternity*

ELENA N. SIFUENTES

Turn to God from Idols
Copyright © 2020 by Elena N. Sifuentes

All Rights Reserved. No Portion of this book may be reproduced, stored in a retrieval system, or transmitted in any form or by any means - electronic, mechanical, photocopy, recording, scanning or other - except for brief quotations in critical reviews or articles, without the prior written permission of the publisher. Subject to permission under action 107 and/or 108 of the 1976 United States Copyright act. Request for permission should be addressed to the publisher elenasifuentes919@gmail.com

First paperback edition July 2020

ISBN - 978-1-7351400-0-1 (paperback)
ISBN - 978-1-7351400-1-8 (eBook)

Published by Elena N. Sifuentes elenasifuentes919@gmail.com

Please note: Every effort has been made to ensure the accuracy of information throughout this book. The information is believed to be accurate at the time of printing. The publish and author are not responsible for errors or omissions, for changes to details or the consequences of the readers reliance to the information provide.

Readers are welcome to contact the publisher for comments, updates or questions.

DEDICATION

This book is dedicated to God Almighty, I am thankful to be a part of His family, an heir. I am thankful for His guidance, love, mercy, grace, and patience; Jesus for his obedience, even death on the cross, so that we would have the assurance of salvation; and for God sending the Holy Spirit our teacher and guide.

To the readers, God yearns for you to accept His Son, Jesus Christ, to bless you and for fellowship with you now and forever.

ACKNOWLEDGEMENT

Thankful for Catherine Olen, my niece, for her guidance and expertise, she is an entrepreneur, writer, and has published numerous books.

Ben L. Wells III (Son) for his continued encouragement throughout this process.

TABLE OF CONTENTS

Dedication iii

Acknowledgement v

Introduction xi

Chapter 1 – The Triune God 1
   God the Father 1
   Jesus, the Son of God 6
   Holy Spirit 12

Chapter 2 – The Bible 15

Chapter 3 – The Lord, Not Idols 20
   Idols 23

Chapter 4 – Idols of the Heart 30
   Physical Idols 31
   Power 40
   Pride 47
   Self-Indulgence 51
   Money 54
   Doubt 63
   Grumbling 68
   Liars and Lying 75

Theft	79
Murder and Anger	82
Fear and Worry	88
Entertainment	95

Chapter 5 – Acts of the Flesh / Earthly Nature... 101

Rivalry	102
Dissension and Division	104
Discord	107
Conflict	111
Hatred/Hate	115
Fits of Rage	119
Factions and Envy	124
Jealousy	128
Drunkenness	131
Folly	134
Lewdness	138
Sexual Immorality, Impurity, and Debauchery	141
Adultery and Lust	148
Evil Desires	152
Greed	156
Orgies	160

Chapter 6 – Test the Lord 165

Chapter 7 – Man's Rules 173
    Traditions 173

Chapter 8 – Foreigners 178
    Temporary Home - World 178

Chapter 9 – Stars, Astrology, Fortune
                telling and Horoscopes....................184
        Naturalism.......................................186

Chapter 10 – Warning...191

Chapter 11 – Spiritual Fullness in Christ...........197

Chapter 12 – Conclusion......................................199

Chapter 13 – Final Note from the Author 203

About the Author..205

INTRODUCTION

A meaningful life

Experiencing a meaningful life can seem like a journey orchestrated over time. Like learning to walk, it does not come overnight; we start by taking baby steps. In the same way, the path to living a Christian life begins by turning to God and striving to live in righteousness by following the guidelines written in the Bible.

My heart desires to encourage everyone to learn the truth about God, especially regarding idols. God is the creator of the heavens and earth, and he is the only one that is omnipotent (unlimited power), omnipresent (everywhere), and omniscient (all-knowing). God is Jehovah-Jireh, which means "The Lord will provide." So, I want you to meet in a personal way, my God, who is all-powerful, all-knowing, and my provider.

Let me start by putting a smile on your face:

> As a child, we often traveled to Mexico to visit our grandmother, dad's mom. On several occasions, the adults, along with our baby brother, went shopping while leaving us three younger children with dad's family. However, I was afraid of "old ladies," as I thought they were all witches. Okay, I don't know where that idea came from, but that's a fact. I sat on the porch, crying because I was afraid, and I refused to go into the house. When the group came back from shopping, I held on to my mom like my life depended on it.

This brings me to the question, where did I get the idea that all old ladies were witches? Was it from a scary movie like the Wizard of Oz, was someone trying to scare me, or were they just pretending and I took them seriously? Just as I needed to learn the truth about elderly ladies, all of us individually need to learn about the truths of the Bible and idols.

Now let's see what the Bible instructs and warns us about worshiping idols so that we can understand what constitutes as an idol to avoid them.

CHAPTER 1

The Triune God

We begin this book with an understanding of what the Bible says about the triune God: God the Father, God the Son, and God the Holy Spirit. Scripture recounts what it means to be obedient and pleasing to God to reciprocate His love for humanity wholeheartedly. The bible teaches the journey of life leads to eternal salvation and heaven. And we need to know why God sent the Holy Spirit to dwell with all of us who love and put their trust in Him. With the foundation of a meaningful Christian Faith now set in place, we can understand how idols are in opposition to the teachings of the Word of God.

God the Father

The Trinity, as recorded in the scriptures, disclose that there is one everlasting God and, at the same time, exist in three persons; God the Father, God the Son, and God the Holy Spirit. Three distinct persons, yet equal as the word of God, accredit all attributes, titles of deity individually to each.

God the Father is the one true God. He is the One who created the universe and rules over everything in it. He knows and loves each of us. He is omnipotent (all-powerful), omniscient (all-knowing), and omnipresent (everywhere). He is the first person of the Trinity, a term meaning "three in one"-the Father, the Son, and the Holy Spirit. In 1Corinthians 1:3, 1 Corinthians 8:6 and 2 Corinthians 1:3, the Bible reveals this truth about God the Father, the Father of our Lord Jesus Christ, the Father of compassion and the God of all comfort:

> *Grace to you and peace from God our Father.*
> *1 Corinthians 1:3*
> *English Standard Version (ESV)*

> *Yet for us, there is but one God, the Father, from whom all things came and for whom we live; and there is but one Lord, Jesus Christ, through whom all things came and through whom we live.*
> *1 Corinthians 8:6*
> *New International Version (NIV)*

TURN TO GOD FROM IDOLS

*Praise be to the God and Father of
our Lord Jesus Christ, the Father of
compassion and the God of all comfort.*
2 Corinthians 1:3
New International Version (NIV)

The first step in a relationship with Almighty God is to love Him with all our hearts. In Matthew 22:36-40, Jesus said the First Commandment is to love the Lord with all our heart, with all our soul, and with all our mind. The story begins with a lawyer trying to tempt Jesus by asking a question based on his understanding of the law:

> *"Master, which is the great commandment in the law?" Jesus said unto him, "Though shall love the Lord thy God with all thy heart, and with all thy soul, and with all thy mind. This is the first and great command and the second is like unto it, Thou shalt love thy neighbor as thyself. On these two commandments hang all the law and the prophets."*
> *Matthew 22:36-40*
> *King James Version (KJV).*

Jesus says one must love the Lord with a sincere heart that is loving Him above all others. We show our commitment to Him by serving and glorifying Him through our actions of kindness, mercy, and love. As a result, we hold Him in adoration, esteem, and with the supreme authority of our fully surrendered lives. We are not to lean on worldly understanding, but instead, we are to transform our minds to the teachings found in the scriptures. God's love for man was demonstrated from the very beginning, making it easier for us to love Him in return. His love is genuine, forgiving, and unconditional. He wants fellowship with us now and through eternity. This is why He sacrificed His only Son on the cross of Calvary. His love is like a father to his children who cherishes, protects, and cares for them. He searches for them like lost sheep, just as a shepherd seeks out his scattered flock, He rescues, cares for them and tends to their needs. We find an illustration of how important His children are to Him in the *Parable of the Lost Sheep found in Luke 15:4-7*:

> *Then Jesus told them this parable: "Suppose one of you has a hundred sheep and loses one of them. Doesn't he leave the ninety-nine in the open country and go after the lost sheep until he finds it? And when he finds it, he joyfully puts it on his shoulders and goes home. Then he calls his friends and neighbors together and says, 'Rejoice with me; I have found my lost sheep.' I tell you that in the same way, there will be more rejoicing in heaven over one sinner who repents than over ninety-nine righteous persons who do not need to repent."*
> *Luke 15:4-7*
> *New International Version (NIV)*

The Second Commandment says we are to love and care for fellow believers above ones-selves. We do this to glorify God and build His Kingdom. God enables us through His grace and empowerment to unselfishly love ourselves and to compassionately love our fellow believers. Through the Holy Spirit, which dwells within us, and by reading the word, God strengthens us to love as Jesus has commanded us to do. Not only does God command His fellow believers to love others, but it pleases Him when He sees a brother in need attended to by a fellow believer. This kind of love extends to the point that one is willing to give up his life for another. Here are two scriptures in which Jesus commands our love for another recorded in John 15:12-17 and John 4:21:

> *My command is this: Love each other as I have loved you. Greater love has no one than this: to lay down one's life for one's friends. You are my friends if you do what I command. I no longer call you servants because a servant does not know his master's business. Instead, I have called you friends, for everything that I learned from my Father I have made known to you. You did not choose me, but I chose you and appointed you so that you might go and bear fruit — fruit that will last — and so that whatever you ask in my name the Father will give you. This is my command: Love each other.*
> *John 15:12-13 and 17*
> *New International Version (NIV)*

> *And this commandment we have from him: whoever loves God must also love his brother.*
> *John 4:21*
> *English Standard Version (ESV)*13

Jesus, the Son of God

Jesus is the Son of God and the second person of the Trinity. He pre-existed as God but became man. The ministry and existence of Jesus were foretold in the Old Testament, and the fulfillment is recorded in the New Testament. According to Apostle John, he referred to Jesus as the 'Word'; the Greek word *logos was used,* which means the spoken word and Jesus is God's spoken word. Throughout the Bible, Jesus was called by many names; among them were Immanuel, God, Word, Lord, Savior, Messiah, and Lamb of God. John 1:1-3 records this amazing transition:

> *In the beginning, was the Word, and the Word was with God, and the Word was God. He was with God in the beginning. Through him, all things were made; without him, nothing was made that has been made.*
> *John 1:1-3*
> *New International Version (NIV)*

Jesus' coming into the world as a man to minister and teach the gospel of His death and resurrection was predicted in Psalm 40:6-8. In this Psalm, David was referring to the redemption of Christ; and the prediction is found in Psalm 118:17-18. In Hebrews 10:5-10 the apostle was quoting what was written in Psalm 40:9-6-8 and Luke 24:5-7, we see the fulfillment:

TURN TO GOD FROM IDOLS

Sacrifice and offering you did not desire – but my ears you have opened – Burnt offerings and sin offerings you did not require. Then I said, "Here I am, I have come – It is written about me in the scroll. I desire to do your will, my God; Your law is within my heart."
Psalm 40:6-8
New International Version (NIV)

I will not die but live, and will proclaim what the Lord has done. The Lord has chastened me severely, but he has not given me over to death.
Psalm 118:17-18
New International Version (NIV)

Therefore, when Christ came into the world, he said: "Sacrifice and offering you did not desire, but a body you prepared for me; with burnt offerings and sin offerings, you were not pleased. Then I said, 'Here I am – it is written about me in the scroll – I have come to do your will, my God.'"
Hebrew 10:5-10
New International Version (NIV)

In their fright, the women bowed down with their faces to the ground, but the men said to them, "Why do you look for the living among the dead? He is not here; he has risen! Remember how he told you, while he was still with you in Galilee: "The Son of Man must

> *be delivered over to the hands of sinners, be crucified and on the third day be raised again."*
> *Luke 23:5-7*
> *New International Version (NIV)*

Isaiah 7:14 foretells of Jesus' birth to a virgin, and He would be called Immanuel, which means God with us. And this fulfillment of His birth is found in Matthew 1:23 and Luke 2:4-7a & 10:

> *Therefore, the Lord himself will give you a sign: The virgin will conceive and give birth to a son, and will call him Immanuel.*
> *Isaiah 7:14*
> *New International Version (NIV)*

> *"The virgin will conceive and give birth to a son, and they will call him Immanuel." (which means "God with us").*
> *Matthew 1:23*
> *New International Version (NIV)*

> *So Joseph also went up from the town of Nazareth in Galilee to Judea, to Bethlehem, the town of David, because he belonged to the house and line of David. He went there to register with Mary, who was pledged to be married to him and was expecting a child. While they were there, the time came for the baby to be born, and she gave birth to her firstborn, a son.* [10]*But the angel said to them, "Do not be afraid. I bring you good news that will cause great joy for all the people.*

TURN TO GOD FROM IDOLS

> *Today in the town of David, a Savior has been*
> *born to you; he is the Messiah, the Lord.*
> *Luke 2:4-7a & 10*
> *New International Version (NIV)*

Jesus was anointed by the Holy Spirit to preach with wisdom, the good news to the poor, bind up the brokenhearted, to proclaim freedom for the captives and release from darkness the prisoners. This was foretold in Isaiah 11:2 and Isiah 61:1-2. The fulfillment and description of the events are recorded in Mark 1:9-10:

> *The Spirit of the Lord will rest on him – the*
> *Spirit of wisdom and of understanding, the*
> *Spirit of counsel and of might, the Spirit*
> *of the knowledge and fear of the Lord*
> *Isaiah 11:2*
> *New International Version (NIV)*

> *The Spirit of the Sovereign Lord is on*
> *me because the Lord has anointed me to*
> *preach good news to the poor. He has*
> *sent me to bind up the brokenhearted,*
> *to proclaim freedom for the captives and*
> *release from darkness for the prisoners.*
> *Isaiah 61:1-2*
> *New International Version (NIV)*

> *At that time Jesus came from Nazareth in*
> *Galilee and was baptized by John in the*
> *Jordan. Just as Jesus was coming up out of*

> *the water, he saw heaven being torn open and*
> *the Spirit descending on him like a dove.*
> *Mark 1:9-10*
> *New International Version (NIV)*

Crucifying lawbreakers was a form of execution used for the worst criminals, a sinner's death. Even though Jesus was without sin and had not warrant such a brutal and horrendous way of execution, it was foretold in the Old Testament. Also, to speed up the death of the ones crucified, the soldiers would break their bones, but since Jesus had already died, they did not break His bones as was foretold in Psalm 22:16-17. The fulfillment is found in Matthew 26:2 and John 19:32-33:

> *Dogs surround me, a pack of villains*
> *encircles me; they pierce my hands and*
> *my feet. All my bones are on display;*
> *people stare and gloat over me.*
> *Psalm 22:16-17*
> *New International Version (NIV)*

> *As you know, the Passover is two*
> *days away — and the Son of Man will*
> *be handed over to be crucified."*
> *Matthew 26:2*
> *New International Version (NIV)*

> *The soldiers therefore came and broke the legs*
> *of the first man who had been crucified with*
> *Jesus, and then those of the other. But when*

> *they came to Jesus and found that he was
> already dead, they did not break his legs.*
> *John 19:32-33*
> *New International Version (NIV)*

Today, Jesus is seated at the right hand of God, a place of honor, as was foretold in Colossians 3:1-2 and the fulfillment is found in Hebrews 3:1 and Hebrews 12:2:

> *Since then, you have been raised with Christ,
> set your hearts on things above, where Christ
> is, seated at the right hand of God. Set your
> minds on things above, not on earthly things.*
> *Colossians 3:1-2*
> *New International Version (NIV)*

> *Since then, you have been raised with Christ,
> set your hearts on things above, where
> Christ is, seated at the right hand of God.*
> *Hebrews 3:1*
> *New International Version (NIV)*

> *Looking to Jesus, the founder and perfecter of
> our faith, who for the joy that was set before him
> endured the cross, despising the shame, and is
> seated at the right hand of the throne of God.*
> *Hebrews 12:2*
> *English Standard Version (ESV)*

Jesus demonstrated His love for us by His obedience to die on the cross so that we can have the assurance of eternal salvation; and at the same time have a personal relationship with God. Our goal, while in this temporary home, called earth, is to strive to live a righteous life so we can enjoy fellowship with God now and forever. Just as Jesus demonstrated, we are to live with a heart of compassion, peace, patience, love, gratefulness, and thanksgiving.

Holy Spirit

The Holy Spirit is the third person of the Trinity and fully God. Another name given to the Holy Spirit is the Helper. In John 14:26, we see the Holy Spirit as the Helper, a teacher as He gives wise counsel:

> *"But the Helper, the Holy Spirit, whom the Father will send in my name, he will teach you all things and bring to your remembrance all that I have said to you."*
> *John 14:26*
> *English Standard Version (ESV)*

In John 16:7-11 and John 13-14, Jesus explains the purpose for sending the Holy Spirit. The Holy Spirit is our guide into all truths; He will convict the world concerning sin, righteousness, and judgment:

> *Nevertheless, I (Jesus) tell you the truth: it is to your advantage that I go away, for if I do not go away, the Helper will not come to you. But if I go, I will send him to you. And when he comes,*

> *he will convict the world concerning sin and righteousness and judgment: concerning sin, because they do not believe in me; concerning righteousness, because I go to the Father, and you will see me no longer; concerning judgment because the ruler of this world is judged. When the Spirit of truth comes, he will guide you into all the truth, for he will not speak on his own authority, but whatever he hears he will speak, and he will declare to you the things that are to come. He will glorify Me, for he will take what is mine and declare it to you.*
> *John 16:7-11 and John 13-14*
> *English Standard Version (ESV).*

Other names given to The Holy Spirit are Comforter, Advocate, Intercessor-Counselor, Strengthener, and Standby. Standby is referring to the Holy Spirit waiting for His children to ask Him for assistance in times of need for comfort or guidance, basically for whatever or whenever a need arises. The Spirit helps us in our weakness as He intercedes for God's people through wordless groans. When Jesus died and rose, God sent a representative in His place, the Holy Spirit. He was not only a teacher, but He was to bring to remembrance what Jesus taught His disciples.

The Holy Spirit was sent for encouragement, to give His followers confidence, and reassurance to proclaim the gospel. The Holy Spirit was to clarify all things, including the doctrine of the Trinity, the Father, the Son, and the Holy Spirit as one unit. He was to teach them things Jesus knew they would not understand and were not prepared to hear while Jesus was with them. This enabled them to preach with confidence the good news to the Gentiles.

When Jesus said, in Matthew 22:36-40, that on these two commandments hang the law and the prophets, He was saying these principals are for instructing people to love God and to love one another as He commanded. These are the foundation of the Ten Commandments. If we keep these two commandments that Jesus gave us, we will be able to keep all the Commandments and the law. For example, if we love our neighbor, we will not covet, steal, murder, or bear false witness against him. The Bible is the rule, and we are commanded to every truth in it.

> *"Master, which is the great commandment in the law?" Jesus said unto him, "Though shall love the Lord thy God with all thy heart, and with all thy soul, and with all thy mind. This is the first and great command and the second is like unto it, Thou shalt love thy neighbor as thyself. On these two commandments hang all the law and the prophets."*
> *Matthew 22:36-40*
> *King James Version (KJV).*

CHAPTER 2

The Bible

The teachings of the Bible are inspired by God and were written by men. There are 40 authors of the Bible; among is the more notable, including David, Moses, Solomon, Matthew, Mark, Luke, John, and Paul. The Bible says that these writers were inspired by God. The Apostle Paul wrote in 1 Corinthians 14-37 that the Lord commanded him what to write:

> *The things I am writing to you*
> *are a command of the Lord.*
> *1 Corinthians 14:37*
> *English Standard Version (ESV)*

In 2 Timothy 3:16, Paul states, "All Scripture is God-breathed and is useful for teaching, rebuking, correcting and training in righteousness.

"This is the only use in the Bible of the Greek word *theopneustos*, which means "God-breathed, inspired by God, due to the inspiration of God," but other scriptural passages support the basic premise of Scripture being inspired by God.[1]

> *All scripture is given by inspiration of God and is profitable for doctrine, for reproof, for correction, for instruction in righteousness*
> *2 Timothy 3:16*
> *King James Version (KJV)*

Jeremiah was a prophet of God, and his work was extended over the nations and kingdoms, a prophet for a world-wide ministry. In Jeremiah 1:9, we read how Prophet Jeremiah expresses how God's inspiration was revealed to him in a more personal way when God touched his mouth and spoke to him:

> *Then the Lord put out his hand and touched my mouth. And the Lord said to me, "Behold, I have put my words in your mouth. See, I have set you this day over nations and over kingdoms, to pluck up and to break down, to destroy and to overthrow, to build and to plant."*
> *Jeremiah 1:9*
> *English Standard Version (NIV)*

Studying the Bible builds faith and trust in God, and it is essential to our proclamation of divine

---

[1] https://www.gotquestions.org/God-breathed.html

truths. In Romans 10:17 and Romans 10:14, we are reminded that faith comes from hearing the word. The importance of spreading the good news is that others who had not heard the message can believe.

> *So faith comes from hearing and*
> *hearing through the word of Christ.*
> *Romans 10:17*
> *English Standard Version (ESV)*

> *How then will they call on him in whom they*
> *have not believed? And how are they to believe*
> *in him of whom they have never heard?*
> *Romans 10:14*
> *English Standard Version (ESV).*

James 1:22-27 is a reminder not just to be hearers of the word but also to be doer by our action of mercy and by staying away from sinful worldly ways.

> *But be doers of the word, and not hearers only,*
> *deceiving yourselves. For if anyone is a hearer*
> *of the word: and not a doer, he is like a man who*
> *looks intently at his natural face in a mirror.*
> *For he looks at himself and goes away and at*
> *once forgets what he was like. But the one who*
> *looks into the perfect law, the law of liberty, and*
> *perseveres, being no hearer who forgets but a*
> *doer who acts, he will be blessed in his doing.*
> *If anyone thinks he is religious and does not*
> *bridle his tongue but deceives his heart, this*
> *person's religion is worthless. Religion that is*
> *pure and undefiled before God the Father is this:*

*to visit orphans and widows in their affliction
and to keep oneself unstained from the world.*
James 1:22-27
English Standard Version (ESV)

The Bible was written as our daily guidebook for righteous living, as we strive to follow its teachings. I say striving because no one is perfect, and we all have stumbling blocks that hinder the Christian walk of obedience. Therefore, we work towards righteousness through reading the scriptures and also by meditating, praying, and in fellowship with other believers.

The Bible also warns us of the consequences of sin. Rejecting Jesus can lead to eternal death if we do not repent. We are to develop a personal relationship with our Lord and Savior. If we do not want to continue sinning, then we need God's help through Jesus and the power of the Holy Spirit.

Throughout the Bible, we read how God, our Creator wants to have a special relationship with His children. He wants us to know Him, and also to trust Him in our daily life and for eternity. We should continuously examine ourselves to see if we have created an idol in our life. This is so important because we cannot worship God and idol at the same time. The scripture says we cannot serve two masters. God wants us to worship Him as our creator, and not His creation. Reading the Bible helps us focus our eyes on heaven. Because, as we read in Philippians 3:20 and, 1 Peter 1:4, our citizenship is in heaven:

> *Our citizenship is in heaven.*
> *Philippians 3:20*
> *New International Version (NIV)*

> *And into an inheritance that can never*
> *perish, spoil or fade. This inheritance*
> *is kept in heaven for you.*
> *1 Peter 1:4*
> *New International Version (NIV)*

CHAPTER 3

The Lord, Not Idols

If we bow down to an image or person other than God, we are bowing down to an idol. An idol is anyone or anything that is worshiped, in which one places trust, faith, hope, and love, over a relationship and allegiance to God.

In Isaiah 44:9-20, Prophet Isaiah explains the process, thoughts, and foolishness of those who make false idols:

> *All who make idols are nothing, and the things they treasure are worthless. Those who would speak up for them are blind; they are ignorant, to their own shame. Who shapes a god and casts an idol, which can profit nothing? People who do that will be put to shame; such craftsmen are only human beings. Let them all come together and take their stand; they will be brought down to terror and shame. The blacksmith takes a tool and works with it in the coals; he shapes*

TURN TO GOD FROM IDOLS

an idol with hammers; he forges it with the might of his arm. He gets hungry and loses his strength; he drinks no water and grows faint. The carpenter measures with a line and makes an outline with a marker; he roughs it out with chisels and marks it with compasses. He shapes it in human form, human form in all its glory,

that it may dwell in a shrine. He cut down cedars or perhaps took a cypress or oak. He let it grow among the trees of the forest, or planted a pine, and the rain made it grow. It is used as fuel for burning; some of it he takes and warms himself, he kindles a fire and bakes bread. But he also fashions a god and worships it; he makes an idol and bows down to it. Half of the wood

he burns in the fire; over it, he prepares his meal, he roasts his meat and eats his fill. He also warms himself and says, "Ah! I am warm; I see the fire." From the rest, he makes a god, his idol; he bows down to it and worships. He prays to it and says, "Save me! You are my god!" They know nothing, they understand nothing; their eyes are plastered over so they cannot see, and their minds closed so they cannot understand. No one stops to think; no one has the knowledge or understanding to say, "Half of it I used for fuel; I even baked bread over its coals, I roasted meat, and I ate. Shall I make a detestable thing from what is left? Shall I bow down to a block of wood?" Such a person feeds on ashes; a deluded heart misleads him; he cannot save himself, or say, "Is not this thing in my right hand a lie?"

Isaiah 44: 9-20

New International Version (NIV)

Turning to God from idols is not easy to do. Furthermore, it is not just something pagans do. We find ancient practice mentioned in Genesis 31:19 when Rachel stole her father's idols. In reality, people follow idols today as a means to focus on their deity or self, another person they have elevated to be an idol or another god.

> *When Laban had gone to shear his*
> *flock, then Rachel stole the household*
> *idols that were her father's.*
> Genesis 31:19
> New American Standard Bible (NASB)

In modern society, people do not simply worship idols made of stone, metal, or wood. Idols can be created easily through new technology, which can provide the means for promoting idols, without realizing that one may be following an idol. The media exposes patterns of living, which can sway one's way of thinking. People are told to be more tolerant and opened minded by considering other religions that do not follow the teachings of the Bible. Instead, one must be vigilant to decipher truth from false teachings.

Recently, while flying to visit my son, I met a woman on the plane from a different faith who repeatedly told me I should consider other religions and be opened minded about it. Whatever I said to her, she would not acknowledge. Yet, at the end of the flight, she mentioned she did not plan to go back to her church. We know people are searching for meaning and purpose for their life. They can start with reading the Bible and then search for a good Bible-teaching church in their neighborhood.

Idols

Some idols were created with the intent to get closer to God, not necessarily to worship the idol. People drew pictures of older men with a beard, draped in robes, or fashioned after other men to visually relate to God. Others worship and pray to the image hoping it would hear their prayers. This description of what people thought God looked like came from the Bible, wherein Genesis 1:26 God said, "Let us make man in our image.

> *Then God said, "Let us make man in*
> *our image, after our likeness."*
> *Genesis 1:26*
> *English Standard Version (ESV).*

Since no one has seen God, no one can imagine the physical likeness of God. Those pictures came out of mans' imagination; therefore, those images can not honestly portray God. The inability to see God is written in the book of Exodus 33:20:

> *"You cannot see my face, for man*
> *shall not see me and live."*
> *Exodus 33:20*
> *English Standard Version (ESV)*

In ancient times smaller images were carved small enough to hold onto easily. During difficult times, these small idols gave their worshippers comfort and security. Skillful craftsmen, such as blacksmith and carpenters, build idols resembling or fashioned after people they worshiped. Modern tools, like power carving or shaving tools, did not exist, so blacksmiths used coal and hammers, while carpenters used chisels. Creating impressive-looking images was slow and meticulous processes, especially high-quality creations worthy of being display in shrines.

Definition and Bible Verses regarding Idols:

The Definition of Idolatry

Idolatry means the "worship of an idol," also known as a "cult image," in the form of a physical image such as a "statue" or "an icon.[2]"

Idolatry is defined by Merrimack Webster as:

1. The worship of a physical object as a god.
2. Immoderate attachment or devotion to something[3]

Another definition of idolatry, according to Merrimack Webster, is:

---

[2] https://en.m.wikipedia.org/wiki/Idolatry
[3] https://www.merriam-webster.com/dictionary/idolatry

"The worship of idols or excessive devotion to, or reverence for some person or thing." An idol is anything that replaces the one, true God. The most prevalent form of idolatry in Bible times was the worship of images that were thought to embody the various pagan deities.[4]

References to the words "idol or idolatry" appear over 40 times throughout the Bible. The Bible gives specific guidance regarding and against worshiping idols. Here are a few verses to help us understand what the scriptures say and worn us about idol worship.

You shall have no other gods before me.
Exodus 20:3
English Standard Version (ESV)

Do not turn to idols or make for yourself any gods of cast metal: I am the Lord your God.
Leviticus 19:4
English Standard Version (ESV)

You shall not make idols for yourselves or erect an image or pillar, and you shall not set up a figured stone in your land to bow down to it, for I am the Lord your God.
Leviticus 26:1
English Standard Version (ESV)

---

[4] https://www.merriam-webster.com/dictionary/idolatry

But their idols are silver and gold, made by human hands. They have mouths, but cannot speak, eyes, but cannot see. They have ears, but cannot hear, noses, but cannot smell. They have hands but cannot feel feet but cannot walk, nor can they utter a sound with their throats. Those who make them will be like them, and so will all who trust in them.
Psalm 115:4
New International Version (NIV)

The idols of the heathen are silver and gold, the work of men's hands. They have mouths, but they speak not; eyes have they, but they see not; They have ears, but they hear not; neither is there any breath in their mouths.
Psalm 135:15-17
King James Version (KJV)

Instead, you have set yourself up against the Lord of heaven. You had the goblets from his temple brought to you, and you and your nobles, your wives, and your concubines drank wine from them. You praised the gods of silver and gold, of bronze, iron, wood, and stone, which cannot see or hear or understand. But you did not honor the God who holds in his hand your life and all your ways.
Daniel 5:23
New International Version (NIV)

Those who pay regard to vain idols forsake their hope of steadfast love.
Jonah 2:8
English Standard Version (ESV)

TURN TO GOD FROM IDOLS

Therefore, my dear friends, flee from idolatry.
I Corinthians 10:14
New International Version (NIV 1984)

Formerly, when you did not know
God, you were enslaved to those
that by nature are not gods.
Galatians 4:8
English Standard Version (ESV)

The acts of the flesh are obvious: sexual immorality, impurity, and debauchery; idolatry and witchcraft; hatred, discord, jealousy, fits of rage, selfish ambition, dissensions, factions, and envy; drunkenness, orgies, and the like. I warn you, as I did before, that those who live like this will not inherit the kingdom of God.
Galatians 5:19:21
New International Version (NIV)

Put to death, therefore, whatever belongs to your earthly nature: sexual immorality, impurity, lust, evil desires, and greed, which is idolatry.
Colossians 3:5 New International Version (NIV)

Dear children, keep yourselves from idols.
I John 5:21
New International Version (NIV)

The rest of mankind who were not killed by these plagues still did not repent of the work of their hands; they did not stop worshiping

> *demons, and idols of gold, silver, bronze, stone,*
> *and wood — idols that cannot see or hear or walk.*
> *Revelations 9:20*
> *New International Version (NIV).*

We can see from these and other verses not referenced here, both in the Old and New Testament, the Bible strongly warns us against idols. When subjects such as these, are mentioned more than once, God is emphasizing the importance of them.

Idols come in a variety of disguises and labels. Initially, we might think of idols as physical creations like a statue or person that one worships that goes back for many centuries. These physical images or statues included animals and people as idols of worship. However, idols are not always made from material items. It can be something or someone other than God, elevated to be a god people worship. People, from other faiths, often believe that idols have power. Hinduism people believe power is hidden in any object:

> An idol or an image is a living embodiment (arca) of God. It is not a lifeless form. Life is poured into every image or idol when it is reverentially worshipped with devotion. Devotion has such power. According to our Puranas, with devotion, you can awaken the divine power

which is hidden in any object. Even the man-made images, though prepared out of inanimate substances, can become 'alive' if they are duly consecrated through the prescribed rites. God, who is omnipotent 'descends' into such images with a subtle body. This is the 'arcāvatāra' or incarnation for purposes of ordinary worship.[5]

---

[5] https://www.hinduwebsite.com/idols.asp

CHAPTER 4

Idols of the Heart

There are many different types of idols, such as idols of the heart, which are stumbling blocks set before us, as crafted idols. We are warned of the consequences of turning to idols of the heart, according to Ezekiel 14:3 and Ezekiel 14:7-8.

> *Son of man, these men have set up*
> *idols in their hearts and put wicked*
> *stumbling blocks before their faces.*
> *Should I let them inquire of me at all?*
> *Ezekiel 14:3*
> *New International Version (NIV)*

> *When any Israelite or any alien living in*
> *Israel separates himself from me and sets*
> *up idols in his heart and puts a wicked*
> *stumbling block before his face and then goes*
> *to a prophet to inquire of me, I the Lord will*
> *answer him myself. I will set my face against*
> *that man and make him an example and a*

> *byword. I will cut him off from my people.*
> *Then you will know that I am the Lord.*
> Ezekiel 14:7-8
> *New International Version (NIV 1984)*

If we are not careful, the following can become an Idol of the Heart: Physical Idols, Power, Pride, Self-Indulgence, Money, Doubt, Grumbling, Liars and Lying, Theft, Murder and Anger, Fear, Worry and Entertainment.

Physical Idols

Exodus 20:3-6 warns that the penalty of idol worshippers does not end with us; instead, it extends to the third and fourth generation for those that hate God. But for those that love and obey God, He extends His love to a thousand generations.

> *You shall not make for yourself an image in the form of anything in heaven above or on the earth beneath or in the waters below. You shall not bow down to them or worship them; for I, the Lord your God, am a jealous God, punishing the children for the sin of the parents to the third and fourth generation of those who hate me, but showing love to a thousand generations of those who love me and keep my commandments.*
> Exodus 20:3-6
> *New International Version (NIV)*

This is reason enough to study and understand what constitutes idol worship. Children have fallen away from the Godly teachings and beliefs taught by their parents and previous family generations. Franklin Graham, son of evangelist Billy Graham, grew up with evangelical parents but stepped away deciding he wanted to be free, have fun, and raise hell. At the age of 22, he returned to faith in God and accepted Jesus Christ as his personal Savior. Today his ministry, Samaritan's Purse is working worldwide, helping people in the areas that have been devastated by violent forces of nature. Just as Franklin Graham, it is time for all those who have fallen away from biblical teachings to return to their faith in God. God wants his children no matter where you're in life.

Jesus came into the world to save sinners. The choice for his people was made even before the creation of the world. God does not step away, but rebellious people choose to turn their backs on God. When one decides to step away from God, it is usually triggered by the struggles of life. God sees the struggles, and He has made a way to return through Jesus' crucifixion and resurrection. If not taught about the consequences of worshiping idols, it is time to break away from worshiping idols to protect yourselves and your future generations. God has empowered His children to be able to break the chains of sin. If worshiping idols, stop using the excuse that, this is how we were brought up, as we are responsible for our own decisions and consequences.

An idol can be anything that keeps us away from our relationship with God. Graven images were carved idols used to worship gods and goddesses. People also use crystals, charms, or stones as part of their beliefs in a higher power.

A rabbit foot dates its origin back to 600 BC. During that time, it was to help with fertility. Today, a rabbit's foot is used in the hope of bringing good luck. I traveled to Ireland, and while I was there, I saw many shamrocks packaged for sale with the title "Luck of the Irish." St. Patrick introduced the little plant back in 433 AD. Also, the authentic "Blarney Luck Stone" was used to give the gift of gab to anyone who kissed it. People climb the steep steps of the Blarney Castle located near Cork, Ireland to kiss the Blarney stone. This act allegedly gave them an eloquent, clever, or flattering speech.

People believe stones and crystals have mystical powers that provide healing. Unfortunately, credit for positive results is given to the object created by God rather than to God, the creator. Other people use stones in cleaning rituals, cleaning them in ways that the powers are not interrupted or minimized. This attempts to limits God's power so they can control their own lives. Unfortunately, they are looking for help in many other places other than God.

Alcohol and drugs should be considered as idols as they affect our thought. When out of control, one does not think of God nor have a personal relationship with God. It is sad to see how the uses of alcohol, drugs, and even prescription drugs have gotten out of control. People are dying because they accidentally overdose or use drugs to commit suicide. Often some people use drugs to find "happiness" and to be on the "top of the world." Instead, they become addicted, depressed, which often leads to suicide. People may start to drink or use drugs socially with business associates, friends, and family but then later find themselves addicted. Perhaps they drink in the hopes of drowning their blues away or fighting stress. I've heard people say, "I need a drink," to give them the courage to complete an activity or calm them before a presentation. It is sad to see someone who has overindulged, only to wake up the following morning feeling miserable, sick with a headache, vomiting, or with a hangover.

Our nation has been blessed abundantly with wonderful things such as a house with a roof over our head to keep us sheltered from harsh climates; clothing to keep us warm or fashionable; jobs and money to purchase all our necessities of life. But sadly, we transfer our focus and attention to these items and forget God is the one that provided them. God wants us to enjoy His blessing and to give thanks to Him for all he has provided. He is the provider of all we need, and He generously showers His children, this is stated in Philippians 4:19:

> *But my God shall supply all your need*
> *according to his riches in glory by Christ Jesus.*
> *Philippians 4:19*
> *King James Version (KJV)*

Other materials can become idols in our lives, such as compulsive uses of smartphones or electronic notebook tablets, computers, televisions, or even a motor vehicle that results in a worshipful attitude that can also feed our pride and ego.

- Smartphones or electronic notebook tablets are popular because they keep us continuously connected to all the calls and text messages we would otherwise miss. Sometimes the use of these devices becomes an addiction. When visiting family or friends, we do not put these electronic devices down to make time to communicate with each other. My friend has a rule that when you visit her, the electronic devices are to be removed and left in a basket near the front door. Phone distractions and obsession have caused many automobile accidents, especially when texting and driving at the same time. The tragic results are often severe injuries and even deaths.

- Excessive watching of television can affect our lives when we set aside responsibilities, especially when they require immediate attention. When television series, a soap opera, a game, a show or a movie is more important, we often say we will do the job later, or maybe it doesn't get done at all. This reminds me of an event that happened when I was just a young girl. One of my favorite movies was Shirley Temple's *Heidi* in a 1937 film. In this film, Heidi is played by Shirley Temple, who was taken away from her grandfather to become a companion to a spoiled disabled girl. Heidi goes through many trials until she is finally reunited back with her grandfather. The movie aired on television on a Sunday morning and I had to make a decision, Do I watch Shirley Temple or do I go to church? I decided to go to church because I wanted to do the right thing. This may not seem to be a significant example; however, as a young person, it was an important decision I needed to make. As we get older, responsibilities and decisions become more complex. Therefore, it is important to make it a habit to make good decisions in obedience to God. It is when we are young, we can start living our lives focused on righteousness so that it can become a good habit.

TURN TO GOD FROM IDOLS

A vehicle can become an idol when we put all our attention and energy into caring for it and abandon others. Many years ago, while on jury duty, I served on a case involving a young man who worshiped his car. He became temperamental when others would just touch his car. Thus, He would fight anyone who wouldn't get away from it because the car was more important to him than anyone and anything. Unfortunately, he took his obsession too far, and he was arrested when he swung a knife, slashing another young man across the neck (fortunately, the young man was not seriously injured). The judge understood this young man's intention and gave him a second chance by ordering him to obtain counseling as part of his punishment. The judge ruled this way because he perceived that the young man had not thoughtfully meditated murder. The young man intended to just protect his idol. Just as the judge gave him a second chance, our Heavenly Father gives us a second chance and often many chances. God does this because He loves us, and He does not want anyone to perish.

Celebrities, sports figures, or entertainers can become idols, and people will show their support by decorating their houses with their memorabilia. We find pleasure and emotional attachment to material objects that remind us of enjoyable times. Fanatics go to every game or show whenever possible. When people physically or orally defend their team isn't that an excessive obsession with things that function like idol worship? Once, at a football game, someone dropped a football cap from one team, and someone from the opposing team stomped on it. This upset fans, and the exchange of negative words resulted. People stood ready to fight, but fortunately, cooler heads prevailed, and everyone moved on. In life's arena, was that act or action all that important?

Celebrities can become an idol if people worship them as many do. Here are a few examples of celebrities virtually worshiped:

- In the 1960s, the English rock band, "The Beatles" whose singers were John Lennon, Paul McCartney, George Harrison, and Ringo Starr, were worshiped by fanatical fans, which was called Beatlemania. Newscasters reported that adolescent girls waited as early as 6:00 in the morning just for a glimpse of them. The Beatles' popularity grew into hysteria and high-pitched fans screaming while the Beatles were traveling or at their concerts. In an interview John Lennon said,

    "We're more popular than Jesus now; I don't know which will go first—rock 'n' roll or Christianity." —"John Lennon to journalist Maureen Cleave."[6]

---

[6] https://en.m.wikipedia.org/wiki/The_Beatles

- Another famous American celebrity, singer and actor, was Elvis Presley. He was successful in so many music arenas, such as pop, country, blues, and gospel music. Many fans referred to him as the "King of Rock and Roll" or the "King." To become an idol, one must be worshiped. In an article printed in Urban Faith, *"Some People Worshiped Elvis Presley as a God"* written by Dr. Melvin Banks. He wrote:

  Back in the day, reports spread that fans of Elvis Presley worshiped him–the king of rock– as a god. Pockets of his worshipers would gather in places like New York, Colorado, and Indiana. They would raise their hands, spell out and then chant Elvis' name, work themselves into a fervor, and then pray to the dead music star.[7]

However, like my good friend, some people were just fans and decorated their houses with Elvis' memorabilia. She did not worship him but enjoyed listening and watching his performances.

---

[7] https://urbanfaith.com/2013/06/some-people-worshiped-elvis-presley-as-a-god.html/

- Michael Jackson was another American singer, songwriter, and dancer who was called the "King of Pop." He was known around the world as one of the most popular entertainers ever. His career started as a child performing with his family. His popularity as a soloist in music began in the early 1980s. In the True discipleship, "*Michael Jackson or God?*" by Richard Holleman reported:

> "It is safe to say that Michael Jackson was not a humble man. He was the epitome of pride, arrogance, self-centeredness, and grandiose feelings. People worshiped him as a virtual God.[8]

Power

Beginning with the book of Genesis, God's power is demonstrated. Almighty God has unlimited power and authority over all, and there is no other person with such power. His power is immeasurably more than imaginable. Reference to God's power is found in Ephesians 3:20, Psalms 37:17, Psalms 37:33, and 2 Corinthians 12:9:

---

[8] https://truediscipleship.com/michael-jackson-or-god/

TURN TO GOD FROM IDOLS

Now to him who is able to do immeasurably more than all we ask or imagine, according to his power that is at work within us, to him be glory in the church and in Christ Jesus throughout all generations, forever and ever! Amen.
Ephesians 3:20
New International Version (NIV).

For the power of the wicked will be broken, but the Lord upholds the righteous.
Psalms 37:17
New International Version (NIV)

But the Lord will not leave them in the power of the wicked or let them be condemned when brought to trial.
Psalms 37:33
NewInternational Version (NIV)

But he said to me, "My grace is sufficient for you, for my power is made perfect in weakness."
2 Corinthians 12:9
NewInternational Version (NIV)

Definition of power:

1. Ability to act or produce an effect
2. Ability to get extra-base hits
3. Capacity for being acted upon or undergoing an effect

Legal or official authority, capacity, or right possession or control, authority, or influence over others

One having such power; specifically: a sovereign state

A controlling group: establishment—often used in the phrase the powers

Archaic: a force of armed men

Chiefly dialectal: a large number or quantity

Physical might

Mental or moral efficacy

Political control or influence[9]

God reveals His power towards His children as He protects them from the snares of the wicked. We don't always get the opportunity to see how God answers our prayers when someone is abusive or disrespectful to us. But we know that God protects His children so we can be confident that He has our back. God knows how to punish people because he knows what is important to them and more effective. In Romans 12:19, we are not to take revenge, and in Proverbs 24:17, we are not to boast over others' disciplinary consequences:

> *"It is mine to avenge; I will repay, says the Lord."*
> *Romans 12:19*
> New International Version (NIV).

---

[9] https://www.merriam-webster.com/dictionary/power

TURN TO GOD FROM IDOLS

> *Do not gloat when your enemy falls;*
> *when they stumble, do not let your heart*
> *rejoice, or the Lord will see and disapprove*
> *and turn his wrath away from them.*
> *Proverbs 24:17*
> *New International Version (NIV)*

Two of my favorite stories in the Bible, showing God's power, protection, and deliverance for His children when His children are faithful to Him, are found in the book of Daniel. These stories are a good example in Psalms 37: 33, where the Lord protected them from the snares of the wicked. In both of these stories, the men were saved, and neither of them was harmed:

> *But the Lord will not leave them in*
> *the power of the wicked or let them be*
> *condemned when brought to trial.*
> *Psalms 37:33*
> *New International Version (NIV)*

1. Daniel was promoted to a position as a high-ranking officer in the Persian Medes Empire. His authority decreed by King Darius over the satraps caused jealousy. This is a case of a successful Jew versus non-Jews. King Darius was tricked into writing a decree, stating that for 30 days, no one was to pray to anyone except him. Daniel trusted, worshiped, and prayed only to God; his only King was Yahweh. Because he stayed faithful

to God, not conforming to the decree set by Darius because of his jealous rivals, he was thrown into the lion's den. But God sent His angels to shut the mouths of the lions, and they did not hurt Daniel because of his faithfulness. When Darius saw this, he was delighted to see that Daniel was saved. So, Darius issued a new decree to all his subjects in the kingdom to fear and reverence the God of Daniel. (Daniel 6)

2. The second story is about three Hebrew men who refused to bow down to the king, so they were thrown into a fiery furnace, heated seven times hotter than normal, by Nebuchadnezzar, King of Babylon. The three men, Shadrach, Meshach, and Abednego, were saved from the fire when the King looked inside the furnace, he saw four men walking around, unharmed in flames and one looked like the Son of God. Not only were they unharmed because of their faithfulness to God, but the king promoted them to leadership positions in the province of Babylon. King Nebuchadnezzar issued a decree that if anyone said anything against their God, they would be cut into pieces and their houses would be turned into rubble. (Daniel 3)

TURN TO GOD FROM IDOLS

The pursuit of power can become an idol when one has an obsession to control others, especially if they abuse others and misuse it to make themselves appear better or more important. Threats that others appear better are a source of insecurity and fear, which causes jealousy. Therefore, they will do anything to be on top, and thus power becomes their idol. A jealous person may willfully hurt others by making the other person feel inferior. An easy way to make someone feel inferior is by not acknowledging their accomplishments when given the opportunity. Abusing power comes with consequences even though it may seem that these people are on top and cannot be destroyed.

Let me tell you about two work experiences, where I observed how two employees took advantage of their authority:

> An employee was promoted to a supervisor's position. Immediately, she showed favoritism towards some employees while showing a lack of concern for others. She developed a superiority attitude and belittling others in her department. Finally, several employees went over her head and took the supervisor's problems to the attention of management.

In response to these charges, Senior Management investigated the supervisor's performance and behavior. They exercised special care to ensure the investigation was done properly and legally. Following their conclusion, the supervisor was counseled to make specific changes in her attitude and management style. She was strongly advised to conform to company policies guidelines, which were mainly to treat all employees fairly, equally, and with respect. However, following this reprimand, the supervisor continued to treat her subordinates in an abasement manner. Subsequently, she was removed from her position.

On another occasion, while I was in training to become a Loan Officer, an Operations Officer stood in the corner, arms folded across her chest, observing employees making sure they were working. She hovered over the employees as if she was a military officer. Her behavior toward other employees was abusive. Again, several employees went to to the administrators, asking them to step in. They called her in, after conducting an investigation, and counseled her to make changes on how she treated employees. However, she did not make the changes she was told to do, and she was removed from her position.

Pride

In these verses, Psalm 10:4, Psalms 73:6-7 and Romans 12:16, pride can become an idol, because some people hold the importance of self above all or reject God:

> *In the pride of his face, the wicked does not seek him; all his thoughts are, "There is no God."*
> *Psalm 10:4*
> *English Standard Version (ESV)*

> *Therefore, pride is their necklace; they clothe themselves with violence. From their callous hearts comes iniquity; their evil imaginations have no limits.*
> *Psalms 73:6-7*
> *New International Version (NIV)*

> *Live in harmony with one another. Do not
> be proud, but be willing to associate with
> people of low position. Do not be conceited.*
> Romans 12:16
> *New International Version (NIV)*

The definition of Pride as taken from the Webster dictionary:

> n The quality or state of being proud; in inordinate self-esteem; an unreasonable conceit of one's own superiority and talents, beauty, wealth, rank, etc., Which manifests itself in lofty airs, distance, reserve, and often in contempt of others

> v To indulge in pride or self-esteem; to rate highly; to plume; use reflexively.[10]

In Ephesians 4, we are instructed to be humble:

> *Be completely humble and gentle; be
> patient, bearing with one another in love.*
> Ephesians 4:2
> *New International Version (NIV).*

Prideful people often need to be in the center of attention. This can be a stumbling block and opens doors for pride to turn into idolatry. They may be self-centered, conceited, pretentious, arrogant, and see themselves as superior.

---

[10] http://www.webster-dictionary.org/definition/Pride

TURN TO GOD FROM IDOLS

Prideful people may not be aware of their weakness because others have allowed them to act this way while growing up, and it has become a way of life. Because of their arrogance, they feel they are above others and cannot learn from them. Working hard to achieve goals gives them the attitude of entitlement. Prideful people may not acknowledge or give credit to achievements that others have accomplished. They do not have a servant's heart and, therefore, do not help others. If they are in a position of authority, they often see themselves as above menial tasks such as manual labor. To make themselves appear superior over others, they will often point fingers revealing others' faults.

Since they do not acknowledge that they make mistakes, they will blame others and not take responsibility for their actions. The Bible instructs us not to be proud but to be humble. James 4:6 reveals that God disapproves the proud but shows favor to the humble; Matthew 23:12 reminds us that those who exalt themselves will be humbled. Luke 14:10-11 reveal that it is better to humble ourselves to allow others to bring us to a place of honor:

> *But He gives us more grace. That is why*
> *Scripture says: "God opposes the proud*
> *but shows favor to the humble."*
> *James 4:6*
> *New International Version (NIV)*

*For those who exalt themselves will
be humbled, and those who humble
themselves will be exalted.*
*Matthew 23:12
New International Version (NIV)*

*But when you are invited, take the lowest
place, so that when your host comes, he will
say to you, 'Friend, move up to a better place.'
Then you will be honored in the presence
of all the other guests. For all those who
exalt themselves will be humbled, and those
who humble themselves will be exalted."*
*Luke 14:10-11
New International Version (NIV)*

Prideful people often feel they are self-sufficient and therefore do not need God or any other person in their life to accomplish their goals. In many cases, these people may appear to be helpful or friendly but instead will stab you in the back to achieve their intended goal. In one of the banks where I worked, the position for an assistant manager was being negotiated. Two individuals were working in the bank that felt they qualified and should get the promotion. One of the employees wanted the promotion to the extent she would hurt others to make herself appear worthy and the best candidate. In part, to hurt others, she would not give an appropriate annual review to employees. She deliberately omitted the accomplishment they made and gave them a lower review grade. She did this to help keep the competition down, especially if she felt they were a threat. This command comes from Proverbs 3:27:

> *Do not withhold good from those who deserve*
> *it, when it is in your power to act...*
> Proverbs 3:27
> New International Version (NIV).

Also, she would take credit for jobs others had done, and eventually, she got caught. This opposes the word of God, as lying and cheating are not acceptable practices. We are to trust God in our daily lives, be honest, and work diligently. We are to show brotherly love as God is the rewarder of good deeds. When we deceive, we are only hurting ourselves because in this case, she missed out on opportunities.

Self-Indulgence

We are to seek the Kingdom of God and His righteousness above all, see Matthew 6:33:

> *But seek ye first the kingdom of God*
> *and his righteousness, and all these*
> *things shall be added unto you.*
> Matthew 6:33
> King James Version (KJV)

When self-indulgence becomes the number one objective in our life, it can be considered an idol of the heart. When we seek excessive gratification to the point that we will do just about anything to satisfy our drives for riches and success, we end up putting ourselves above others, see Philippians 2:4 and Philippians 2:21. Desiring talents solely for self-gratification can demonstrate a selfish heart, see James 3:14-16. Our attitude should be to use our abilities to entertain, encourage, witness, or lighten someone else's burden. This is not to say that our talents are only to be used in a church or Christian setting as God uses us in different places and different ways to reach out to the lost. The venue is never the issue but our intention, which comes from our heart's desire.

> *Let each of you look not only to his own interests but also to the interests of others.*
> *Philippians 2:4*
> *English Standard Version (ESV)*

> *For they all seek their own interests, not those of Jesus Christ.*
> *Philippians 2:21*
> *English Standard Version (ESV)*

> *But if you have bitter jealousy and selfish ambition in your hearts, do not boast and be false to the truth. This is not the wisdom that comes down from above but is earthly, unspiritual, demonic. For where jealousy and selfish ambition exist, there will be disorder and every vile practice.*
> *James 3:14-16*
> *English Standard Version (ESV)*

TURN TO GOD FROM IDOLS

We are instructed in Colossians 3:17 to do everything in the name of Jesus and with a grateful heart:

> *And whatever you do, whether by speech or action, do everything in the name of the Lord Jesus, giving thanks to God the Father through him.*
> Colossians 3:17
> *International Standard Version (NIV)*

The definition of self-indulgence is:

> Excessive or unrestrained gratification of one's own appetites, desires, or whims[11]

Television programs can play a significant part by influencing one's thoughts to be happy, fulfill dreams, and to be on top of the world. A couple of programs that can influence these thoughts are: *The Ninja Warrior UK* and *Dancing with the stars*. Everyone desires to achieve the "American Dream" to be acknowledged as the best or to be the star that people look up to. These programs can influence us to think, "How wonderful it would be if I could only be the strongest contestant and finish the goal in record time or be the best dancer." Are we seeking self-gratification as thinking that is the only way to fulfill our desires,

---

[11] https://www.merriam-webster.com/dictionary/self-indulgence

dreams, or to be happy, and does God get any credit? Now accomplishing these goals is not the issue, and when someone wins, it should be with a thankful heart. The issue is when the focus is put solely on self-indulgence, taking all the credit. Sure, we have to work hard, but this is only possible because God gives us the ability and talents to accomplish set goals. These achievements should be used to glorify God by how we handle ourselves, graciously accepting the given reward. The exhortation of ourselves should only come from others as we are to humble ourselves before the Lord, see James 4:10:

> Humble ourselves before the
> Lord, and he will exalt us.
> *James 4: 10*
> *English Standard Version (ESV)*

The opposite of selfishness as found in Philippians 2:4 (see above). We should be sincere with a willing heart to relinquish our belongings, to spend for the salvation of souls or deny ourselves, and to always be ready for whatever advances the Kingdom of God.

Money

The subject of money has been tossed, stating that the wealthy hoard money or are stingy. They are accused of robbing others by using their influence and money to buy favors or get their way. Even though there may be some validity to this, too often, the negative is verbalized while others secretly donate generously. Matthew 6:4 states that we should give in private as our heavenly Father will reward us:

> *Give Your gifts in private, and your Father,*
> *who sees everything, will reward you.*
> *Matthew 6:4*
> *New Living Translation (NLT)*

God provides for all our needs as He knows our needs before we even ask of Him and He gives blessings out of His riches so that we can accomplish our missions according to His will, see Philippians 4:19 and 2 Corinthians 9:8

> *And my God will supply every need*
> *of yours according to his riches in*
> *glory in Christ Jesus.*
> *Philippians 4:19*
> *English Standard Version (ESV)*

> *And God is able to bless you abundantly, so*
> *that in all things at all times, having all that*
> *you need, you will abound in every good work.*
> *2 Corinthians 9:8*
> *New International Version (NIV)*

We can only have one master as it is impossible to serve or give allegiance to two masters wholeheartedly. If money becomes your sole focus in life, then you cannot serve God. See Matthew 6:24:

> *"No one can serve two masters, for either he will hate the one and love the other, or he will be devoted to the one and despise the other. You cannot serve God and money."*
> *Matthew 6:24*
> *English Standard Version (ESV).*

The bible instructs us not to love money but to be content with what God provides. God is our provider, and He will always be with us, ready to give a helping hand. We are to keep our focus on God's purposes and not to hoard money for self-gratification. We are not to put our hope in money, but on God, money is the root of all kinds of evils. See Hebrews 13:5, Luke 12:34, 1 Timothy 6:17 and 1 Timothy 6:9-10:

> *Keep your life free from love of money and be content with what you have, for he has said, "I will never leave you nor forsake you."*
> *Hebrews 13:5*
> *English Standards Version (ESV)*

> *For where your treasure is, there your heart will be also.*
> *Luke 12:34*
> *New International Version (NIV)*

> *Command those who are rich in this present world not to be arrogant nor to put their hope in wealth, which is so uncertain, but to*

*put their hope in God, who richly provides
us with everything for our enjoyment.*
1 Timothy 6:17
New International Version (NIV)

*For the love of money is a root of all
kinds of evil. Some people, eager for
money, have wandered from the faith and
pierced themselves with many griefs.*
*1 Timothy 6:9-10 New
International Version (NIV)*

The Definition of money:

Plural- moneys or monies: Something generally accepted as a medium of exchange, a measure of value, or a means of payment: such as:

1. a : officially coined or stamped metal currency newly minted money
   b: money of account
   c: paper money handed the bank teller a wad of money
2. a: wealth reckoned in terms of money made her money in the insurance business
   b: an amount of money raised the money for a new library
   c: moneys or monies plural: sums of money: funds the collection of tax monies
3. a form or denomination of coin or paper money wanted his money in $10 bills[12]

---

[12] https://www.merriam-webster.com/dictionary/money

When thinking about money, our first question should be, " Who is the provider?" In Philippians 4:19 (see above), we see that God can supply all our needs. Jehovah Jireh is the Hebrew word, which means, "The Lord will provide" or "The Lord will see to it."God is omniscient (all-knowing) He is aware of our needs, and He generously provides.

When I was 17, I was shy and lacked confidence. One of my sisters asked me if I wanted to work. So my first thoughts were, "I guess so" and "If they were smart, they would hire somebody else. But I'm going to do my best whether I make it or not, at least I know I tried and did my best". Time passed by, and I was offered opportunities, and I took them as I felt that if others thought I could do the job, then I should at least try. In case you are wondering, I realize that God gave me abilities I didn't know I had, and He opened doors of opportunities through my life's journey. Also, I took business classes, and one thing I learned was the importance of saving for the future. The instructor advised about putting money into 401(k) as he explained that even a little goes a long way over time. I believe that God was looking out for me even before I realized it, as he has provided for my needs. It could be so easy for me to say I did a great job, but I know better, see Deuteronomy 8:17-18:

> *You may say to yourself, "My power and the strength of my hands have produced this wealth*

*for me." But remember the Lord your God, for
it is he who gives you the ability to produce
wealth, and so confirms his covenant, which
he swore to your ancestors, as it is today.*
Deuteronomy 8:17-18
New International Version (NIV).

Work is a gift from God as He gives us the skills and talents needed to be successful in whatever job we choose. He provides for our needs, money to invest, and money to assist the needy. All jobs, roles, and skills are equal in the eyes of God as He uses all of us to accomplish His plan. We are to glorify God through our devotion to Him and looking to him for leadership, strength, and wisdom.

Having money is not the problem, but it is our attitude towards it that can make it an idol. The scriptures instruct that if we worship money, we cannot worship God because we cannot have two masters, money, and God. However, we are to honor the Lord with our wealth as He has directed in Proverbs 3:9:

*Honor the Lord with your wealth and with
the first fruits of all your produce; then
your barns will be filled with plenty, and
your vats will be bursting with wine.*
Proverbs 3:9
English Standard Version (ESV)

We need to be contented with what we have as God knows exactly what we need, and he is our provider. In Act 8:18-24, Simon thought he could give Peter money in exchange for the power of laying hands on others to receive the Holy Spirit, but since it was a gift from God, it was not possible, so Perter reprimanded Simon because his heart was not right with God.

> *When Simon saw that the Spirit was given at the laying on of the apostles' hands, he offered them money and said, "Give me also this ability so that everyone on whom I lay my hands may receive the Holy Spirit." Peter answered: "May your money perish with you because you thought you could buy the gift of God with money! You have no part or share in this ministry because your heart is not right before God. Repent of this wickedness and pray to the Lord in the hope that he may forgive you for having such a thought in your heart. For I see that you are full of bitterness and captive to sin." Then Simon answered, "Pray to the Lord for me so that nothing you have said may happen to me."*
> *Acts 8:18-24*
> *New International Version (NIV)*

When Jesus was talking to his followers, he was not condemning them, especially the wealthy, but He was trying to impress on them that they could not buy their way into heaven. He told them that they did not have the means to get into heaven on their own. If one's focus' is entirely on being rich, one needs to be aware of the consequences of it

TURN TO GOD FROM IDOLS

disappearing, according to the Berean Study Bible Proverbs 23:5:

> Berean Study Bible Proverbs 23: 5: Saying 8 "4 Do not wear yourself out to get rich; be wise enough to restrain yourself. 5 When you glance at wealth, it disappears, for it makes wings for itself and flies like an eagle to the sky". [13]

Even though we are not to weary ourselves out by working, we are not to be lazy and not work, or we can become poverty-stricken, see Proverbs 14:23:

> *In all toil there is profit, but mere talk tends only to poverty. The crown of the wise is their wealth, but the folly of fools brings folly.*
> *Proverbs 14:23*
> *English Standard Version (ESV)*

A principle for living regarding money is always to pay a fair price when hiring someone. By paying a fair price, we are protecting ourselves from becoming greedy, and at the same time, we are obedient to God. This principle is found in Jeremiah 22:13:

> *"Woe to him who builds his house by unrighteousness, and his upper rooms by*

---

[13] https://biblehub.com/bsb/proverbs/23.htm

> *injustice, who makes his neighbor serve him*
> *for nothing and does not give him his wages."*
> *Jeremiah 22:13*
> *English Standard Version (ESV)*

We are instructed not to exploit those that work for us but to be generously conducting our affairs with justice, see Psalms 112:5:

> *It is well with the man who deals*
> *generously and lends; who conducts his*
> *affairs with justice.*
> *Psalms 112:5*
> *English Standard Version (ESV)*

I visited a church, and the pastor preached that for God to answer our prayers, we were required to give an offering. Trying to buy favors from God, in this case, caused money to become an idol as this goes against God's word. We are to ask and then wait for God to answer as Luke states in Matthew 7:7:

> *"Ask, and it shall be given you; seek,*
> *and ye shall find; knock, and it shall be*
> *opened unto you: For every one that asketh*
> *receiveth; and he that seeketh findeth, and*
> *to him that knocketh it shall be opened."*
> *Matthew 7:7-8*
> *King James Version (KJV)*

Salvation is a gift from God because of Jesus' death on the cross. He once and for all paid the price through His death on the cross. We cannot pay for any favors or salvation, nor can we earn them with good works. God wants our fellowship now and through eternity, and He wants us to live a blessed life. In Acts 8:20-23, we see how Peter responded to Simon, wanting to buy power:

> *But Peter said to him, "May your silver perish with you because you thought you could obtain the gift of God with money! You have neither part nor lot in this matter, for your heart is not right before God. Repent, therefore, of this wickedness of yours, and pray to the Lord that, if possible, the intent of your heart may be forgiven you...."*
> *Acts 8:20-23*
> *English Standard Version (ESV)*

Doubt

Our prayers are not always answered the way we wish, partly because of our lack of faith that something will happen. We pray but doubt that God wouldn't answer because we do not feel worthy. In a world of opposing views towards Christianity, the believers can find it difficult not to fall into the trap of doubt. When we ask and allow God to help us overcome doubt, He provides a way for our chains of doubt to be removed forever. We are to have faith and not doubt as God commands in the James 1:6-7 and Matthew 14:29-31:

> *But when you ask, you must believe and not doubt, because the one who doubts is like a wave of the sea, blown and tossed by the wind. That person should not expect to receive anything from the Lord.*
> *James 1:6-7*
> *New International Version (NIV)*

> *"Come," he said. Then Peter got down out of the boat, walked on the water, and came toward Jesus. But when he saw the wind, he was afraid and, beginning to sink, cried out, "Lord, save me!" Immediately, Jesus reached out his hand and caught him. "You of little faith," he said, "why did you doubt?"*
> *Matthew 14:29-31*
> *New International Version (NIV)*

Definition of Doubt:

noun

- 1. a feeling of uncertainty or lack of conviction:
  "some doubt has been cast upon the authenticity of this account."
  Synonyms: uncertainty, lack of certainty, unsureness, indecision, hesitation, ... more
  antonyms: certainty, conviction, confidence, trust

verb

- 1. feel uncertain about:
  "I doubt my ability to do the job."
- 2. fear; be afraid:
  "I doubt not your contradictions."[14]

Doubt, especially when it pertains to something that cannot be seen, heard, or touched, causes a lack of conviction that something is true. Without the facts, it is hard to have faith in someone or things like religious beliefs. Often, we are afraid or cast suspicion on what we hear or see, so we either step away or research its validity. When someone preaches, and you doubt what they say, the Holy Spirit may be nudging you to check it in the Bible to know what is correct. We need to learn and memorize scripture to be prepared and not be misguided by false teaching.

When I think of doubt, the first thing that comes to mind is disciple Thomas, the doubter, because he had to see the wounds, he touches Jesus where the nails pierced his hands, and also had to touch His side before he would believe that Jesus had returned to earth after His death and resurrection, seen in John 20:24-25:

> *Now Thomas (also known as Didymus), one of the Twelve, was not with the disciples when Jesus came. So the other disciples told him,*

---

[14] https://www.google.com/search?client=safari&rls=en&q=define+doubt&ie=UTF-8&oe=UTF-8

> *"We have seen the Lord!" But he said to them, "Unless I see the nail marks in his hands and put my finger where the nails were, and put my hand into his side, I will not believe."*
> *John 20:24-25*
> *New International Version (NIV).*

In Matthew 14:29-31 (see above), when Peter kept his eyes on Jesus, even while in the wind-blown tossed Sea of Galilee, he displayed his courage by stepping out to meet Jesus. Even though the circumstance may be frightening, the key is to keep your eyes on Jesus. When we begin to doubt, that means that we are no longer relying on God, we are allowing fear to enter into our thoughts. Therefore, when Peter set his focus on the roaring of the wind and waves, he became afraid and began to sink. Just as Jesus reached out to Peter and saved him, Jesus reaches out to save us in time of trials.

Another person that doubted was Zachariah. In Luke 1:18-20, we see doubt demonstrated when Zachariah did not believe his elderly wife, Elizabeth, who was going to have a son when the angel Gabriel announced the good news. So he was silenced until the child was born.

> *Zechariah asked the angel, "How can I be sure of this? I am an old man and my wife is well along in years." The angel said to him, "I am Gabriel. I stand in the presence of God, and I have been sent to speak to you and to tell you*

TURN TO GOD FROM IDOLS

> *this good news. And now you will be silent*
> *and not able to speak until the day this happens*
> *because you did not believe my words, which*
> *will come true at their appointed time."*
> *Luke 1:18-20*
> *New International Version (NIV).*

In my research, I came across this article about doubt and idolatry and felt it was worth sharing. Gregory A. Boyd explains doubt, and this information comes from his book Benefit of the Doubt and from the blog by Rachel Held Evans, September 17, 2013, "In the book, I make the case that we are created with a core need to feel fully alive, unconditionally loved and worthwhile, and ultimately secure, and God created us with this need because He wants to meet it, and is the only one who can meet it. An idol, I argue, is anything we use in place of God to meet this core need. While many people try to meet this need with the idols of wealth, power, success, sex, and other things, many Christians try to meet it with the idol of certainty-seeking faith. The quest to feel certain need becomes an idol when a person's sense of significance to God and security before God is anchored not in their simple trust of God's character, as revealed on the cross, but in how certain they feel about the rightness of their beliefs. This form of idolatry is a danger whenever people assume (rightly) that they are saved by faith while also (mistakenly) equating faith with their sense of certainty. For it means they now feel "saved"

– uniquely significant and secure before God – based on their psychological certainty."

As I show in Benefit of the Doubt, the only way to get free from this without falling into some other form of idolatry is to realize that biblical faith isn't about feeling certain, but about a willingness to commit to living for God in the face of uncertainty. We need to accept that uncertainty is simply part of what it means to be human and to trust that God's love for us, revealed most perfectly on Calvary, isn't dependent on how certain or uncertain we feel. The God revealed on Calvary isn't a God who is impressed with people's ability to make themselves feel certain that their beliefs are right. He's rather a God who simply wants us to trust him, in the face of uncertainty, by lovingly laying down our lives for him in response to the way he has lovingly laid down his life for us."[15]

Grumbling

Grumbling and complaining can be an idol because we may be displaying ungratefulness and showing a lack of thanksgiving to God for what he has provided. The following verses recorded in Philippians 2:14, 1 Peter 4:9, Numbers 14:27-28, James 5:9 and 1 Corinthians 10:8-11 commands us not to grumble:

---

[15] https://rachelheldevans.com/blog/greg-boyd-interview-doubt

TURN TO GOD FROM IDOLS

Do everything without grumbling or arguing.
Philippians 2:14
New International Version (NIV)

Offer hospitality to one another
without grumbling.
1 Peter 4:9
International Version (NIV)

How long will this wicked community grumble
against me? I have heard the complaints of
these grumbling Israelites. So tell them, As
surely as I live, declares the Lord, I will do
to you the very thing I heard you say:
Numbers 14:27-28
International Version (NIV)

Don't grumble against one another,
brothers and sisters, or you will be judged.
The Judge is standing at the door!
James 5:9
New International Version (NIV)

We should not commit sexual immorality, as
some of them did – and in one day twenty-three
thousand of them died. We should not test
Christ, as some of them did – and were killed by
snakes. And do not grumble, as some of them
did – and were killed by the destroying angel.
These things happened to them as examples
and were written down as warnings for us, on
whom the culmination of the ages has come.
1 Corinthians 10:8-11
New International Version (NIV)

The Definition of grumbling, according to Merriam Webster:

plural grumblings

1. a mutter of discontent, complaint
2. a growling or reverberating noise, rumbling[16]

The Definition of grumbling according to the Vocabulary Dictionary:

v. make complaining remarks or noises under one's breath, make a low noise, make a certain noise or sound, utter or emit low dull rumbling sounds, express audibly; utter sounds (not necessarily words), show one's unhappiness or critical attitude, or express complaints, discontent, displeasure, or unhappiness

n. a complaint uttered in a low and indistinct tone an expression of grievance or resentment, a loud low, dull, continuous noise. sound of any kind (especially unintelligible or dissonant sound)[17]

---

[16] https://www.merriam-webster.com/dictionary/grumbling
[17] https://www.vocabulary.com/dictionary/grumble

The definition of Complaining from The Free Dictionary:

> complain, complained, complaining, complaints
>
> 1. To express feelings of pain, dissatisfaction, or resentment.
> 2. To make a formal accusation or bring a formal complaint or file a complaint.[18]

Grumbling and discontentment can be expressed by attitudes of impatience or resentment because of jealousy over what others have accomplished. This may stem from jealousy because of an ungrateful heart, especially when we compare ourselves to those that have accomplished more or are prosperous. When we are not thankful, we can end up being miserable as we covet what others have. Once we stop comparing ourselves to others and transfer our focus to what God has provided with a thankful heart, then the grumbling will begin to diminish.

In several books of the Bible, Exodus, Genesis, Leviticus, Numbers, Deuteronomy, and Joshua, we read the story of how the Israelites were rescued from slavery. In Genesis, God made the everlasting covenant to His people to be their God; He heard their cry for help from the hands of Pharaoh,

---

[18] https://www.thefreedictionary.com/complaining

and then He delivered them from their oppression of slavery out of Egypt. During their journey in the desert to the promised land, He would guide them by day with a pillar of clouds and by night with a pillar of fire. He rescued them on dry land, and while crossing the Red Sea, He had caused the sea to separate with a strong east wind. Pharaoh's crew followed the Israelites and were overthrown in the Red Sea when the Lord brought back the water. Psalm 136-15 God overthrew Pharaoh and his army in the Red Sea. Exodus 14:27 also backs this up.

> *But swept Pharaoh and his*
> *army into the Red Sea*
> *Psalms, 136:15*
> *New International Version (NIV)*

> *The water flowed back and covered the*
> *chariots and horsemen – the entire army*
> *of Pharaoh that had followed the Israelites*
> *into the sea. Not one of them survived.*
> *Exodus 14:28*
> *New International Version (NIV)*

God provided for the Israelite's daily provisions. Yet the entire community grumbled against God when they focused on the positive side of living in Egypt compared to the oppression they had. They grumbled because they were reminiscing on the foods they ate while in Egypt, such as fish they wanted, cucumbers, melons, leeks, onions, and garlic. They were ungrateful because God had only given them water and manna, bread from heaven, which they only had to pick up and eat. They grumbled and complained as they did not remember all that God did and was still doing for them by providing for all their needs, protecting them from the outdoor elements, and from all other dangers that could have occurred during their long journey.

Grumbling happens when people feel entitled, and do not remember what God has done and is doing for them, like protecting them daily. To keep away from grumbling or complaining, one needs to focus on God's continuous protection, and this must be done with a grateful heart. Have you ever said, "That was a close call" and thought about what God protected you from, at this point we need to be thankful for God's protection. Once while traveling across from Cardiff Wales to Pembroke Ireland, the weather was frightful, preventing everyone from traveling across the Irish Sea, especially on a ferry, so we were stuck at the port for 12 hours before allowed to travel. Then an elegant looking cruise ship, unlike the little ferry, arrived for us to embark, and then we began our journey towards Pembroke Ireland. I thought, "I wonder, what did God protect us from"? If we knew that answer, 12 hours would seem insignificant.

There are times when complaints are necessary, and there is a right way of handling it; we need to evaluate the purpose of the complaint making sure it is legitimate, and then we need to approach the other person calmly with a positive attitude allowing them to receive the complaint with an open mind. Here is an example of when we may need to express a complaint or need. I am short, and too often, when I go to the market, what I need is way in the back on the top shelf and the last one. So I can complain and say, "Why would they put that on the top shelf, surely everybody needs the item so they should put it down where everyone can reach it." The popularity of the need for the item would be evident by the fact that only one was left. But instead, I look around for a tall person and ask them to get the item down for me. For a short person, this could be a legitimate complaint, but instead, with a smile and a kind word, someone is always ready to give a hand by taking the item down. (I know this is a stretch, but you get the idea).

When not receiving the proper medical care during times of crisis or illnesses, and someone is negligent by not responding to what is needed would be a legitimate time to verbalized a complaint. Hard as it may seem at the time, we need to watch our words and temper.

Liars and Lying

Many verses in the Bible warn us against lying. I have selected several verses about what the Word has to say since God detests this way of life, they are found in Proverbs 6:16-19, Proverbs 12:18-19, Proverbs 12:22, John 8:31-32 and Ephesians 4:15:

> *There are six things the Lord hates, seven that are detestable to him: haughty eyes, a lying tongue, hands that shed innocent blood, a heart that devises wicked schemes, feet that are quick to rush into evil, a false witness who pours out lies and a person who stirs up conflict in the community.*
> *Proverbs 6:16-19*
> *New International Version (NIV)*

> *There is one whose rash words are like sword thrusts, but the tongue of the wise brings healing. Truthful lips endure forever, but a lying tongue is but for a moment.*
> *Proverbs 12:18-19*
> *English Standard Version (ESV)*

> *The Lord detests lying lips, but he delights in people who are trustworthy.*
> *Proverbs 12:22*
> *New International Version (NIV)*

> *To the Jews who had believed him, Jesus said, "If you hold to my teaching, you are*

*really my disciples. Then you will know the
truth, and the truth will set you free."*
John 8:31-32
New International Version (NIV)

*Instead, speaking the truth in love, we will
grow to become in every respect the mature
body of him who is the head, that is, Christ.*
Ephesians 4:15
New International Version (NIV)

The definition of Liars/lying by Urban Dictionary:

1. someone who represents one set of facts, while knowing that a different set of facts prevails;
2. (popular) someone who has led others to believe one thing, does a different thing; a promise-breaker;
3. (colloquial) someone whose general conduct, level of reliability, relationship with the truth, and past performance leave him or her with little to no credibility in peoples' opinion; [19]

Lying becomes an idol because of its selfish intentions to deceive or exaggerate, making someone seem to be something they are not, such as being rich, or talented.

---

[19] https://www.urbandictionary.com/define.php?term=Liar

I have been around people that continually lie and exaggerate deceiving others and making it difficult to know when they are telling the truth. At this point, my mind wanders, and I think, "Are they telling the truth, is this just another story they made up, or are they exaggerating?" When someone is labeled as a liar, it is very difficult to go back and trust them as their words have no credibility. Some people exaggerate the truth to give the appearance that something is greater then what it is, while others practice "little white lies" not wanting to offend others to keep the peace, but when we are not telling the truth, the opposite is lying.

One reason people lie may be an attempt to get others to see them as intelligent, or better, thus making up stories to make themselves appear superior. Defamation of character is another form of lying and is harmful; attacking people's character is never a righteous way of living, and getting others to believe a lie is a form of fraud. Some people lie by omission as they will leave out important information to make someone believe in something that is not true. I've seen representatives trying to sell a product that ended up being inferior, but they build it up to look like a miracle product.

Another form of an idol about lies is when people make promises but do not follow through. They sometimes will promise to do something knowing they have no intention of following through. In Matthew 21:28-31, we read how one son said he would work in the vineyard but then did not keep his word.

> *"What do you think? A man had two sons. And he went to the first and said, 'Son, go and work in the vineyard today.' And he answered, 'I will not,' but afterward he changed his mind and went. And he went to the other son and said the same. And he answered, 'I go, sir,' but did not go. Which of the two did the will of his father?" They said, "The first." Jesus said to them, "Truly, I say to you, the tax collectors and the prostitutes go into the kingdom of God before you."*
> Matthew 21:28-31
> *English Standard Version (ESV)*

In this story, the working in the vineyard is referring to what we are required to do in building up the Kingdom of God. The first son was not willing to be obedient, but then he repented and changed his mind. While the second son was saying that he would obey God but was actually in opposition to the teachings of God. Jesus was trying to get religious leaders in his audience to see that He was referring to them and condemning them because they saw themselves as self-righteous and virtuous. Jesus was referring that some collectors and prostitutes had repented. Still, not the members of the Sanhedrin, the self-righteous ones, so since the collectors and prostitutes repented, they would go into the kingdom of God before Sanhedrin's.

Theft

Seeking to obtain things that do not belong to us without permission of the owner leads to theft and other crimes like murder. Theft becomes an idol when we covet what does not belong to us, and we wrongfully act to obtain it. Putting its importance above all is the result of not seeking God's best for our lives. Now let's see what the scriptures instruct in Hosea 4:2, Proverbs 10:2 and Exodus 22:2-3:

> *There is only cursing, lying and murder,*
> *stealing and adultery; they break all bounds,*
> *and bloodshed follows bloodshed.*
> *Hosea 4:2*
> *New International Version (NIV)*

> *Treasures gained by wickedness do not profit,*
> *but righteousness delivers from death.*
> *Proverbs 10:2*
> *English Standard Version (ESV)*

> *If a thief is found breaking in and is struck so*
> *that he dies, there shall be no bloodguilt for him,*
> *but if the sun has risen on him, there shall be*
> *bloodguilt for him. He shall surely pay. If he*
> *has nothing, then he shall be sold for his theft.*
> *Exodus 22:2-3*
> *English Standard Version (ESV)*

The Definition of theft is:

1. a: the act of stealing; specifically: the felonious taking and removing of personal property with the intent to deprive the rightful owner of it
b: an unlawful taking (as by embezzlement or burglary) of property
2. a stolen base in baseball
3. obsolete: something stolen[20]

Ephesians 4:28 instructs us to stop stealing, get an honest job, and work with our hands, which will enable us to provide for our needs without having to steal. Also, we are to work so that we can share with others and not be a burden but to be a blessing. We are to be responsible, generous, good stewards, and accept opportunities when the doors are opened to work. Stealing can lead to idleness since people that steal usually do not work for a living and are irresponsible people; therefore, money stolen can become an avenue for drugs, lewdness, or liquor.

> *Let the thief no longer steal, but rather*
> *let him labor, doing honest work with*
> *his own hands, so that he may have*
> *something to share with anyone in need.*
> *Ephesians 4:28*
> *English Standard Version (ESV)*

---

[20] https://www.merriam-webster.com/dictionary/theft

TURN TO GOD FROM IDOLS

Theft can be classified as either "Grand theft" which in some states is classified as a felony, and the stolen value must be over the statutory limits set by states or "Petty theft" which is classified as a misdemeanor because the value of the stolen item is less than the statutory value. The differences depend on the magnitude of seriousness, value, and potential consequences. Theft can turn into murder, for example, when someone is killed in a robbery. While living in California, a Liquor Store was robbed, and when the thieves were running away, one of them shot the owner and killed him. Other forms of theft can be by deception also known as fraud, an example of this: there is a scam that has been passed along in which someone will offer and give you a check for double the amount they are asking from you, but the bogus check takes a long time to be routed back to your bank as a fraud. Another form is extortion when someone is coerced into acting involuntarily; someone may threaten you with a weapon or hold a loved one hostage to make you commit a crime.

Here is a story I heard years ago. There was a man that had stolen personal property from his friend; then, he became nervous, stressed, and afraid of being caught, so he kept the stolen items hidden. In this situation, he did not only risked getting caught while stealing the items, but he was afraid that the truth would eventually be revealed. Overwhelmed with the guilt he eventually confessed and returned the items. When I think about this story, I think what a waste of time he spent on worrying and the agony he put himself over trinkets. When honest people are tempted and cave in to the temptation, their conscience can overtake them with guilt.

Murder and Anger

The following scriptures, Matthew 5:21-26, Exodus 20:13, Ephesians 4:31-32, James 1:19-20, Psalms 37:8-9 and Proverbs 15-1 not only refer to murder but also includes anger. In either case, there are consequences that a judge can impose as punishment for these crimes, such as prison time and/or the death penalty. Anger, though not as harsh of a crime as murder, but can result in murder, and they both can become an idol because the intent is a selfish motive.

> *"You have heard that it was said to those of old, 'You shall not murder; and whoever murders will be liable to judgment.' But I say to you that everyone who is angry with his brother will be liable to judgment; whoever insults his brother will be liable to the council; and whoever says, 'You fool!' will be liable to the hell of fire. So if you are offering your gift at the altar and there remember that your brother has something against you, leave your gift there before the altar and go. First, be reconciled to your brother, and then come and offer your*

gift. Come to terms quickly with your accuser while you are going with him to court, lest your accuser hand you over to the judge, and the judge to the guard, and you be put in prison. Truly, I say to you, you will never get out until you have paid the last penny."
Matthew 5:21-26
English Standard Version (ESV)

You shall not murder.
Exodus 20:13
New International Version (NIV)

Let all bitterness and wrath and anger and clamor and slander be put away from you, along with all malice. Be kind to one another, tenderhearted, forgiving one another, as God in Christ forgave you.
Ephesians 4:31-32
English Standard Version (ESV)

Know this, my beloved brothers: let every person be quick to hear, slow to speak, slow to anger; for the anger of man does not produce the righteousness of God.
James 1:19-20
English Standard Version (ESV)

Refrain from anger, and forsake wrath! Fret not yourself; it tends only to evil. For the evildoers shall be cut off, but those who wait for the Lord shall inherit the land.
Psalms 37:8-9
English Standard Version (ESV)

*A soft answer turns away wrath, but
a harsh word stirs up anger.*
Proverbs 15:1
English Standard Version (ESV)

The Definition of murder by dictionary.com is:

> *Law.* The killing of another human being under conditions specifically covered in law. In the U.S., special statutory definitions include murder committed with malice aforethought, characterized by deliberation or premeditation or occurring during the commission of another serious crime, as robbery or arson (first-degree murder), and murder by intent but without deliberation or premeditation (second-degree murder).[21]

In some cases, one party may not be aware of the anger that another party has against them. Therefore, the person with the anger problem is the only one who suffers as this can affect their health. See below the article Every Day Health, which lists seven ways that ager can affect your health.

---

[21] https://www.dictionary.com/browse/murder

Every Day Health list seven ways that anger can affect your health:

"7 Ways Anger Is Ruining Your Health"

1. An angry outburst puts your heart at great risk.
2. Anger ups your stroke risk.
3. It weakens your immune system.
4. Anger problems can make your anxiety worse.
5. Anger is also linked to depression.
6. Hostility can hurt your lungs.
7. Anger can shorten your life.[22]

The best solution is to communicate to resolves the possible misunderstanding as we are directed to reconciliation. I've met hot-tempered people who would speak out before thinking, but if they were made aware of hurting someone, they would apologize. This made me think, are there more mean or nice people? I have read mixed articles regarding the opinion as to whether more people were nice or mean; however, the consensus revealed two views. Some people felt that there are more nice people in the world, but because they are stable, enjoy life, and don't stand out, we don't notice them. However, other people think there are more mean people in the world because they are noticed

---

[22] https://www.everydayhealth.com/news/ways-anger-ruining-your-health/

as they are usually boisterous, obnoxious, and willing to act out their negative behavior.

Murder becomes an idol when someone premeditates and takes action to kill another person. In most cases, murder stems from greed, the need for drugs or alcohol, jealousy, power, or revenge. Overly confident people feel they are too smart to get caught and, thus, are not afraid to take chances so they will kill even if it is for self-gratification. Thrill-seekers will scare their victim before killing them and then gloat over their accomplishments, which also gives them self-gratification.

Victims can be a friend, an acquaintance, or a celebrity that people elevate to the status of an idol, or they just fixate on them seeking a relationship that is not possible. The idol is either not interested in them, or not even aware of them, and perhaps not financially on the same level; therefore, they cannot hope to have a relationship. Unable to succeed in establishing a relationship, they may prefer that if they cannot have them, then no one else should have them. This may be the final factor in deciding for them to murder their idol and themselves falsely hoping to be reconciled with their idol by death.

When I feel betrayed or disappointed, I take it up to the Lord in prayer, as this helps me not to be so angry or anxious. I usually pray for the person or people for God to help them. Also, I give the problem to God and say, "Lord, I put this at your feet" (I may have to do this several times) and also pray, "forgive them for they know not what they do" as Jesus stated in Luke 23:34. Once I've put the problem in God's hands and have calmed down, then I knew I could proceed and deal with the issue at hand. Since our trials are not as harsh as what Jesus went through, and He forgave, we need to follow his example and forgive all our offenders.

> *Jesus said, "Father, forgive them, for they*
> *do not know what they are doing."*
> *Luke 23:34,*
> *New International Version (NIV).*

Jesus' loves is displayed by his willingness to forgive everyone, including those that took part in crucifying Him. He forgave those that tormented, belittled, spat on Him, and even those that hung beside Him on a cross. While preaching on the Mountain, Jesus told his disciple to love their enemies, this is found in Matthew 5:43-44 as Jesus said:

> *"You have heard that it was said, 'You shall*
> *love your neighbor and hate your enemy.'*
> *But I say to you, Love your enemies and*
> *pray for those who persecute you."*
> *Matthew 5:43-44*
> *English Standard Version (ESV).*

Throughout the ages, we have seen that men and women do not think alike; therefore, it is important to try to put ourselves in another person's shoes and ask ourselves, "What did they mean"? Unfortunately, communicating with others has been an issue from the beginning of time, and we need to realize that we may have interpreted something said incorrectly. Here is an example of misinterpreting someone and learning the truth: A group of people gathered to play The Newlywed Game, and the husband was asked if he could pick out how his wife would answer the following question, "What can your wife do better today than she did when you first got married?". The young man answered she would say that she does a better job ordering takeout food. Everyone laughed when the game show host lifted his eyebrows and faced the audience as to question the meaning of his answer. The host replied with a question, "She doesn't know how to cook, so she regularly ordered takeout food"? The husband explained that she knew how to cook, but when they both worked extended hours, it was faster to get take out food, and her choices of food had improved for his liking, and he was complimenting her.

Fear and Worry

In the book of Matthew 6:25-34, Joshua 1:9 and Isaiah 41:10 Jesus is teaching us not to worry but to seek after God and His righteousness, therefore we are not to worry about what we are going to eat, drink and wear as our Heavenly Father already knows what we need and he freely provides. Also, these are words of encouragement to be strong and not afraid. This is a reminder that God will provide for our daily needs because He loves and values us more than we can imagine, so He will not leave us but help us.

> *"Therefore I tell you, do not worry about your life, what you will eat or drink; or about your body, what you will wear. Look at the birds of the air; they do not sow or reap or store away in barns, and yet your heavenly Father feeds them. Are you not much more valuable than they? Is not life more than food and the body more than clothes? Can anyone of you by worrying add a single hour to your life: Therefore do not worry about tomorrow, for tomorrow will worry about itself. Each day has enough trouble of its own."*
> *Matthew 6: 25-34*
> *New International Version (NIV)*

> *Have I not commanded you? Be strong and courageous. Do not be frightened, and do not be dismayed, for the Lord your God is with you wherever you go.*
> *Joshua 1:9*
> *English Standard Version (ESV)*

> *Fear not, for I am with you; be not dismayed, for I am your God; I will strengthen you, I will help you, I will uphold you with my righteous right hand.*
> *Isaiah 41:10*
> *English Standard Version (ESV)*

Definition of Fear by Merriam Webster:

> a: an unpleasant often strong emotion caused by anticipation or awareness of danger
> b: (1) : an instance of this emotion (2) : a state marked by this emotion[23]

Definition of Worry by Your Dictionary:

Noun
1. The definition of worry is something that causes you to feel uneasy or anxious or a troubled state of mind.
   - Not having any money is an example of financial worry.
   - The feeling you experience when you are concerned and nervous about something is an example of worry.
2. Verb
   To worry is defined as to feel anxiety or nervousness. When you are thinking about all the things that could go wrong, this is an example of a situation where you worry.[24]

When we are not keeping our eyes towards God, the circumstance can cause us to become fearful.

---

[23] https://www.merriam-webster.com/dictionary/fear
[24] http://www.yourdictionary.com/worry

TURN TO GOD FROM IDOLS

When we are anticipating danger and afraid and not putting our trust in Him, then fear can become our idol.

Whenever striving to be a perfectionist, people are afraid of making mistakes and end up putting too much pressure on themselves. We need to strive to do our best or achieve high goals, but we need to know our limitations and accept them than living in fear. We all want to achieve goals that make us look good, but when we are putting too much pressure, we end up living in fear of failure. The consequences of living in fear of failure can lead to many illnesses, such as heart attack, high blood pressure, or stroke.

Here are a couple of stories regarding fear:

> Viva, my mom's friend, was a sweet woman that lived within walking distance from us. When I was a little girl, Viva would come over, and they would walk or take a bus to the market. My mom did not drive, and she did not let that get in her way as she would walk whenever needed. Viva was a sweet and caring woman that I perceived to be much older than my mom. My mom was blessed with youthful skin and

looked younger than her age, even in her senior years. During this time, I had the belief that all old ladies were witches, so when they went out, I would pray, "please don't let that old witch hurt my mom." I had worried about what possibly could have happened if she was truly a witch. Even though she was not a witch, I believe that God heard and answered my prayer for protection. We can say that such a nice lady like Viva wouldn't have hurt my mom, but at the same time, we do not know what God may have saved them from, especially since we lived in a rough neighborhood in South Central Los Angeles, California.

As a young lady, while working at a bank as a Loan Officer, one of my responsibilities included ordering financial securities such as government bonds for the upscale customer. New in this position and my first time ordering securities brought fear as I did not have anyone to guide me to make sure I was submitting the order correctly. However, I had our Standard Procedure Manual (SPM), which gave instructions for the various parts of the job, including ordering financial securities. So hesitantly, I read the manual, followed the instructions, and sent the request to our Security Department using the inter-office mail service. Since I was not comfortable in this part of my job, my confidence level was minimal. I was afraid of making a mistake by ordering the wrong securities or not completing the forms correctly. This happened on a Friday so all weekend I worried, couldn't sleep and I was afraid to tell anyone about my dilemma.

Monday morning, the first thing I did when I got to work was to call the Security Department to make sure that the order was completed correctly. I told the gentleman that I had worried the whole weekend, and he said, "Oh, I'm sorry you worried, but you did it correctly."

So, I worried about something that never happened. This could be one of those "what if" situations. What if I had done it incorrectly, it could have been corrected, and this would have been a lesson learned. As a Christian today, I would say, I did my best, I followed the manual, and I trust God gave me wisdom. Whether I did it right or not, it would have been rectified. God's word is calming to my spirit, and after praying, I would have made a choice just to enjoy the weekend and wait until Monday to see the outcome. You know the choice I made whether I thought about it or not was to allow fear and anxiety to control my life.

Fear can be another form of pride because we may be afraid to allow God to control our lives. Following the Lord's guidance at times seems hard or scary; we may hesitate because we are scared of what others may say or how this will affect relationships. When we hold back, we are displaying our need to be in control as we think we don't need anyone's help, or we just don't put our trust in God.

Entertainment

We are instructed in Colossians 3:17 to do everything in the name of the Lord Jesus with thanksgiving. We are to keep in mind the principles God has laid out for us to live a godly life. The Lord created everything so that we could have a blessed life, see James 1:17.

> *And whatever you do, in word or deed, do everything in the name of the Lord Jesus, giving thanks to God the Father through him.*
> *Colossians 3:17*
> *English Standard Version (ESV)*

> *Every good and perfect gift is from above, coming down from the Father of the heavenly lights, who does not change like shifting shadows*
> *James 1:17*
> *New International Version (NIV)*

The definition of entertainment is:

noun
1. The act of entertaining; agreeable occupation for the mind; diversion; amusement: Solving the daily crossword puzzle is an entertainment for many.
2. Something affording pleasure, diversion, or amusement, especially a performance of some kind: The highlight of the ball was an elaborate entertainment.

3. Hospitable provision for the needs and wants of guests.
4. A divertingly adventurous, comic, or picaresque novel.
5. Obsolete. Maintenance in service.[25]

When being entertained, we are not to put a stumbling block in front of those that are weak. When considering someone who is trying to recover from alcoholism, be considerate and do not drink in front of them as this can trigger their desire to drink again. This can also help the alcoholic if no one is drinking, then they will not feel isolated.

A doctor once told a family to "continue serving alcoholic beverages to strengthen the alcoholic to say no when tempted outside the home." This goes against the word of God as we are advised against putting stumbling blocks before people. If someone in the family has a problem with alcohol, we should be more considerate as we can also become an alcoholic. Life is hard enough so we should help each other and not put out stumbling blocks that can cause failure, see Romans 14:13:

> *Therefore let us not pass judgment*
> *on one another any longer, but rather*
> *decide never to put a stumbling block or*
> *hindrance in the way of a brother.*
> *Romans 14:13*
> *English Standard Version (ESV).*

---

[25] https://www.dictionary.com/browse/entertainment

TURN TO GOD FROM IDOLS

In whatever you do for entertainment, do it with a thankful heart. God created all things as he wants us to live an abundant life and to enjoy his creation. From the descriptions taken from the story of the creation as described in the book of Genesis, I envision the Garden of Eden to look like the beautiful countryside. A countryside filled with a combination of beautifully landscaped meadows, a place of serenity, with fruitful trees and a paradise pleasing to the eyes. While traveling through the British Isles, I thought, "this is surely a glimpse of the Garden of Eden. I saw many different shades of green grass and trees, fields covered with numerous sheep and cattle. While watching the sheep, I thought, "The sheep are so peaceful with no worries and so well cared for by their shepherds, just as our Lord God cares for His children." This was a visual picture of a peaceful life and a reminder of how God takes care of his children as He is the Shepherd, and His people are His flock. A reminder of God caring for his children is found in Isaiah 40:11 and Ezekiel 34:15-16:

He tends his flock like a shepherd: He
gathers the lambs in his arms and
carries them close to his heart.
Isaiah 40:11
New International Version

I myself will be the shepherd of my sheep, and
I myself will make them lie down, declares
the Lord God. I will seek the lost, and I will

*bring back the strayed, and I will bind up the
injured, and I will strengthen the weak.*
Ezekiel 34: 15-16
English Standard Version (ESV)

There are limited opportunities to be around the snow in Southern California, but I have been fortunate to visit one of my brothers and sister-in-law when they lived in Seattle. On one occasion, my trip included a visit to Leavenworth, a winter wonderland, located in the Cascade Mountains of Washington. Snow fell the first night of our trip, and I was captivated by the picturesque carpet of snow the following morning, enhancing the charm of Christmas time store decorations. We were blessed on our journey home through a forest magnificently decorated by God.

Then how is it that entertainment can become an idol? When we do not keep entertainment in perspective by neglecting God and our family's best interest. This can happen by participating in activities such as gambling (chasing after riches) and being reckless or irresponsible with our finances. We place stumbling blocks with our finances by not paying bills to pay for such activities and trying to achieve material wealth or recognition to the point we become highly indebted. If we use entertainment as a crutch for comfort or to escape from reality we need to be careful that we are not leaning on entertainment in place of God.

TURN TO GOD FROM IDOLS

Unfortunately, I know several families in which gambling became their Idol. They were addicted to gambling, pursuing the big win, or trying to make just enough money to get back what they lost, and they lost their vision of what was important to them and God. In some cases, they gambled to the point they lost their house, or they lost their family through divorce. I had heard people say that when they gambled, they did not think of their troubles, as they found comfort in gambling.

I went to a party in which alcohol was served, and the two brothers, George and John freely, had too much to drink. They became loud and agitated with the anger of jealousy over feelings that John was loved more than George by their parents. John was accused of taking advantage of their parent's good nature and wealth, which caused the brothers to fight orally. George pulled out a gun, pointing it towards John, but fortunately, the parents were able to cease the fight. The gun was taken away, and George was sent home to cool off. What a tragedy this could have been had George shot his brother. The parents took a stand and decided they had enough, so they got rid of the bar and all the alcoholic beverages.

As you can see, we don't know how we will handle ourselves in a given situation, and the brother did not act responsibly. This is why the Lord warns us against putting ourselves into a situation that can lead to temptation. The parents taking a stand remind me of 1 Peter 3:11-12.

> *Let him turn away from evil and do good;*
> *let him seek peace and pursue it. For the*
> *eyes of the Lord are on the righteous, and his*
> *ears are open to their prayer. But the face*
> *of the Lord is against those who do evil.*
> *1Peter 3:11-12 English Standard Version (ESV)*

Time can be an issue when we put all our time into an activity without regard for others, which includes being a workaholic. Workaholics often put excessive hours at work, avoiding the responsibilities they may have at home or other functions like church. We are to manage our time by being good stewards as we are to balance work, family, entertainment, and always including God.

CHAPTER 5

Acts of the Flesh / Earthly Nature

Other sins that are not considered acts of the flesh are sins outside the body, but these sins are against our own body and are harmful to the extent one can lose the inheritance of the kingdom of God.

> *Now the works of the flesh are evident: sexual immorality, impurity, sensuality, idolatry, sorcery, enmity, strife, jealousy, fits of anger, rivalries, dissensions, divisions, envy, drunkenness, orgies, and things like these. I warn you, as I warned you before, that those who do such things will not inherit the kingdom of God.*
> *Galatians 5:19-21*
> *English Standard Version (ESV)*

> *Put to death, therefore, whatever belongs to your earthly nature: sexual immorality, impurity, lust, evil desires, and greed, which is idolatry.*
> *Colossians 3:5*
> *New International Version (NIV)*

Rivalry

Healthy rivalry can be good when competing in places like sports events such as the *Olympics*, or a singing competition like *The Voice*, and dancing competitions such as *Dancing with the Stars*. These encourage working hard toward higher levels enabling one to achieve goals otherwise unobtainable. When defeated, be a gracious loser by congratulating and enjoy in the well-being of those who accomplish their goals, as they also worked hard. Philippians 2:2-3 reminds us to do nothing from rivalry.

> *Complete my joy by being of the same mind, having the same love, being in full accord and of one mind. Do nothing from rivalry or conceit, but in humility, count others more significant than yourselves.*
> *Philippians 2:2-3*
> *English Standard Version (ESV)*

The definition of rivalry:

> It is the act of competing for the same thing against another person.[26]

Unfortunately, rivalry can become an idol when our focus becomes obsessive in achieving goals with a malicious heart. When ventures get out of hand with the negative motive to achieve the potential goal of being the best or defeating the competitor, people can get hurt. People try to win by eliminating the competition as they may perceive that this will give them a better chance of winning. Football is a good example as players get hurt, but is it accidental or purposely an attempt to win the game? We have seen in the media or at a football game, individuals that show poor sportsmanship, especially among dirty players. One football player said he was doing his job even though he injured his opponent deliberately after the play had ended. His bullying was verified by photos and videos taken of the game. He further complained that he should not have been fined for injuring his opponent because he claimed he was just doing his job. There are consequences for this negative behavior, as seen with this football player. Depending on the offense, football players can be fined with monetary means or get kicked out of the game. This goes against God's desire for

---

[26] https://www.vocabulary.com/dictionary/rivalry

harmony and love of one another for his people. He expects everyone to play fair.

Dissension and Division

In Titus 3:9-11, we are to avoid foolish disagreements because they are unprofitable and worthless. Romans 16:17-18, the Apostle Paul was warning his brothers in Christ to be cautious because some teachers were causing splits and divisions by not following the teaching of Jesus Christ. Paul further told them to avoid their instructions, to peacefully depart from them, and not have fellowship with them. They were not even to meet with them privately; He knew they were not able to discern scriptural truths. Paul was concerned that they could be easily lead astray. This is a good reminder to study the scriptures so that we, too, will not be easily swayed by false teachings.

> *But avoid foolish controversies, genealogies, dissensions, and quarrels about the law, for they are unprofitable and worthless. As for a person who stirs up division, after warning him once and then twice, have nothing more to do with him, knowing that such a person is warped and sinful; he is self-condemned.*
> *Titus 3:9-11*
> *English Standard Version (ESV)*

> *I appeal to you, brothers, to watch out for those who cause divisions and create obstacles*

> *contrary to the doctrine that you have been*
> *taught; avoid them. For such persons do*
> *not serve our Lord Christ, but their own*
> *appetites, and by smooth talk and flattery,*
> *they deceive the hearts of the naive.*
> Romans 16:17-18
> *English Standard Version (ESV)*

The definition of dissension is:

> noun
> 1. Strong disagreement; a contention or quarrel; discord.
> 2. Difference in sentiment or opinion; disagreement.[27]

The definition of division, according to Dictionary.com, is:

> separation by difference of opinion or feeling; disagreement; dissension.[28]

The Scriptures instruct us to be aware and take caution not to be deceived by those that cause dissension and division, especially within the church. None of us will always agree with everything that others may say or do; however, we have a responsibility to express our opinions regarding matters of our belief, but this is not what the scriptures are

---

[27] https://www.dictionary.com/browse/dissension

[28] https://www.dictionary.com/browse/division?s=t

referring to. Dissensions or divisions can become an idol because of the attitude or behavior that leads to divisions within the organization, which goes against the word of God.

Some people want things to go their way no matter what, to the point that they do not accept nor entertain the opinions of others. I have seen where churches have had a split over issues of relocating or refurbishing; one side wanted to relocate to meet the needs of the growing church, while the other side wanted to continue working or tweak the established plans. Both sides sound legitimate, but after all, isn't this the house of the Lord? At this point, both sides should have prayed together to seek the will of God and compromise. Once the vote was made to either relocate or not, those that opposed should have honored the majority vote. Unfortunately, compromise to conclude serving the best interest of the church ended in a split. I am not pointing fingers; however, I wonder what would've happened had those that were contentious or quarrelsome would have stepped aside. Also, in keeping with the scripture in Romans 16:17-18 (see above), those that stirred up division could have been avoided or eliminated from the meetings. Only God sees the whole picture, and we don't know why this situation turned out the way it did, but we are to trust God in every situation as God can use any situation to accomplish his plan.

Another concern may be when there are rules or beliefs stated by the by-laws of some denominations that are challenged or opposed. This can cause dissension where clarification is needed to determine what is correct. We should seek advice and guidance from the elders of the church and the word of God. To please God, our focus should always be on "what would Jesus do or say about this?"

Discord

Proverbs 6:12-15 refer to someone who practices evil by sowing discord as someone wicked and worthless. This scripture also warns that calamity will suddenly appear. Throughout history, we have seen how calamity, events like earthquakes, and storms have come suddenly, causing chaos. Likewise, calamity can come in a blink of an eye to those that devise evil in their heart.

> A worthless person or a wicked man, goes about with crooked speech, winks with his eyes, signals with his feet, points with his finger, with perverted heart devises evil, continually sowing discord; Therefore calamity will come upon him suddenly; In a moment he will be broken beyond healing.
> *Proverbs 6:12-15*
> *English Standard Version (ESV)*

Definition of discord by King James Version (KJV) Dictionary:

> Disagreement among persons or things. Between persons, a difference of opinions; variance; opposition; contention; strife; any disagreement which produces angry passions, contest, disputes, litigation, or war. Discord may exist between families, parties, and nations.[29]

Definition of Discord by Merriam Webster:

> Discord, strife, conflict, contention, dissension, variance mean a state or condition marked by a lack of agreement or harmony. Discord implies an intrinsic or essential lack of harmony producing quarreling, factiousness, or antagonism.[30]

Some people are not happy unless they are arguing. Their attitude can be an idol as they perceive themselves as being all-knowing with the need to have the last word, and whatever they say is right, and everyone else is wrong; they think that others don't know what they're talking about. No matter

---

[29] https://av1611.com/kjbp/kjv-dictionary/discord.html

[30] https://www.merriam-webster.com/dictionary/discord

what one may think, there is no such thing as a perfect person. Only God is omniscient.

I have met people, whether knowingly or not, they come across as know it alls. These people deliberately cause conflict because of their attitude, as they disregard other's opinions or suggestions. When these people are asked questions out of their field of expertise, they will surely have the right answer. For example, ask a non-medical person a question about someone who may have specific symptoms, and they will, from afar, diagnose that person whether they know all the facts or not. Sometimes I want to ask them, "Where did you get your medical degree?" This is not to say that if we have had a medical issue and someone else has the same illness that we cannot help them. Sometimes God allows us to experience illnesses or problems to help others in need.

Wicked people thrive on deceiving and hurting others to the point of ruining reputation by giving false testimony and smearing the other person's name. Also, the wicked thrive on finding anything that seems juicy gossip to report, whether it is true or not, as seen in the media targeting celebrities and people in public. Sadly these people are not remorseful or care at all of what they do, and often they only care about a story they can sell. They are masters of deceiving because they know the right words to use. They may even present themselves as nice or honestly caring about people so that others will freely speak out as a friend. The

Bible reminds us to be watchful, see 1 Peter 5:8 and Matthew 7:15:

> *Be sober-minded; be watchful. Your adversary, the devil, prowls around like a roaring lion, seeking someone to devour.*
> *1 Peter 5:8*
> *English Standard Version (ESV)*

> *Beware of false prophets, who come to you in sheep's clothing but inwardly are ravenous wolves.*
> *Matthew 7:15*
> *English Standard Version (ESV).*

We must be watchful and careful because these people who cause discord can be manipulators; they cannot be trusted; they don't care about anybody but themselves. This is why scripture says that one must be aware of false prophet for they are like wolves in sheep clothing; they disguise themselves to gain confidence in their prey by their smooth and flattering teaching. They want to appear as being gentle by blending in with others; however, when they respond impulsively, they can become dangerous with their plans to devour the flock for their gain. Proverbs 19:1 calls these people fools:

> *Better is a poor person who walks in his integrity than one who is crooked in speech and is a fool.*
> *Proverbs 19:1*
> *English Standard Version (ESV).*

Conflict

Throughout the scriptures, the subject of conflict is mentioned in several verses. The Spirit and flesh conflict with each other, hot-tempered stir up conflict or hatred stir up conflict. The opposite of conflict is peace, and we are to strive for peace whenever possible. See Galatians 5:17, Proverbs 15:18, Proverbs 16:28, Habakkuk 1:3b-4a and Proverbs 10:12:

> *For the flesh desires what is contrary to the Spirit, and the Spirit, what is contrary to the flesh. They are in conflict with each other so that you are not to do whatever you want.*
> *Galatians 5:17*
> *New International Version (NIV)*

> *A hot-tempered person stirs up conflict, but the one who is patient calms a quarrel.*
> *Proverbs 15:18*
> *New International Version (NIV)*

> *A perverse person stirs up conflict, and a gossip separates close friends.*
> *Proverbs 16:28*
> *New International Version (NIV)*

> *Destruction and violence are before me; there is strife, and conflict abounds. Therefore the law is paralyzed, and justice never prevails.*
> *Habakkuk 1:3b-4a*
> *New International Version (NIV)*

*Hatred stirs up conflict, but love
covers over all wrongs.*
Proverbs 10: 12
New International Version (NIV)

Conflict defined as:

1. Uncountable noun [oft in/into N]
    Conflict is a serious disagreement and argument about something important. If two people or groups conflict, they have had a serious disagreement or argument and have not yet reached an agreement.
2. Uncountable noun
    Conflict is a state of mind in which you find it impossible to make a decision.
3. Variable noun
    Conflict is fighting between countries or groups of people.
4. Variable noun
    Conflict is a serious difference between two or more beliefs, ideas, or interests. If two beliefs, ideas, or interests conflict, they are very different.
5. Verb
    If ideas, beliefs, or accounts conflict, they are very different from each other, and it seems impossible for them to exist together or to be true to each other.[31]

---

[31] https://www.collinsdictionary.com/dictionary/english/conflict

TURN TO GOD FROM IDOLS

Conflict becomes an idol because of its nature to stir up serious disagreements that are impossible to be rectified. Thrill or drama seekers feed their ego by causing tension and stir up conflict; this is so that others will see them as powerful, intelligent, and important. Because of a boring or a miserable life, they enjoy watching others feud and enjoy their reactions. Attention seekers are loud, making sure they are heard.

In Romans 12:18, when possible, we are to live in peace with everyone. This means that we need to relinquish our rights to take revenge and forgive the defender. Matthew 6:14 further states if we forgive others, our heavenly Father will forgive us.

In the early 80's I went through a divorce, and even though I forgave my ex-husband, I found myself remembering our wedding each year on our anniversary date. To forget, I prayed that the Lord would take that out of my mind to forgive and forget. In time the date became just another day. See Job:9:27 and Job 11:16.

> *If it is possible, as far as it depends on*
> *you, live at peace with everyone.*
> *Romans 12:18*
> *New International Version (NIV)*

> *For if you forgive other people when*
> *they sin against you, your heavenly*
> *Father will also forgive you. But if you*

> *do not forgive others their sins, your
> Father will not forgive your sins.*
> *Matthew 6:14-15*
> *New International Version (NIV)*

> *If I say, 'I will forget my complaint, I
> will change my expression and smile,'*
> *Job 9:27*
> *New International Version (NIV)*

> *You will surely forget your trouble,
> recalling it only as waters gone by.*
> *Job 11:16*
> *New International Version (NIV)*

Now there are times when it is necessary to confront the offender and the right way to approach them. The right way of handling the offender is explained in Matthew 18:15-17:

> *If our brother sins against you, go and tell him his fault, between you and him alone. If he listens to you, you have gained your brother. But if he does not listen, take one or two others along with you, that every charge may be established by the evidence of two or three witnesses. If he refuses to listen to them, tell it to the church. And if he refuses to listen even to the church, let him be to you as a Gentile and a tax collector.*
> *Matthew 18:15-17*
> *English Standard Version (ESV)*

People can drain our energy, which can become overwhelming, so we will need to step away if all they want to do is engage in an argument or conflict. We are to strive to obtain peace but know when it is time to step away and leave it in the hands of God.

This reminds me of a man that lived across the street from one of the churches I went to in California; he would threaten people and tell them not to park in front of his house and to ensure that other could not park there he began parking his car in the middle so that there was not enough space to park in front or in back of his car. The pastor, along with the elders of the church, would go over to his house and tried to speak to him, but he was not cooperative. It took years with the kindness of the pastor and members of the church until he finally gave in and stopped chasing people away.

Hatred/Hate

People that hate tend to belittle others because they feel threatened. I worked with a girl that outwardly displayed hatred towards others; she expressed her upbringing was difficult, also she was not a happy person, so I found that the only way to work with someone like her is to be kind and stay out of the way. Her hatred and jealousy stemmed from her insecurities. People may say things like, I have your back, but in reality, they cannot be trusted. They will tell you things to present themselves as superior over you.

There is a time to hate, in Psalms 97:10, we are instructed to hate evil, and in Ecclesiastes 3:1-8, there is a time for everything:

> *Let those who love the Lord hate evil.*
> *Psalms 97:10*
> *New International Version (NIV)*

> *There is an appointed time for everything. A time for every activity under the heavens.*
> *Ecclesiastes 3:1, 8*
> *New World Translation (NWT).*

A saying I like to use is, "Hate the sin and pray for the sinner," I take this from 1 Timothy 2:1:

> *First of all, then, I urge that supplications, prayers, intercessions, and thanksgivings be made for all people.*
> *1 Timothy 2:1*
> *English Standard Version (ESV).*

Leviticus 19:17 tells us not to hate our brother but reason frankly with our neighbor to avoid sinning because of him. While in 1 John 2:9-11 if we hate our brother, then we are living in the dark and not living in the light, that is not following God's ways of faith or holiness. Proverbs 10:12 reminds us that hatred stirs up strife, that awakens old feuds, while love covers all offenses. When we forgive, we are also to forget and not bring up old conflicts, remove all bitterness as stated in Ephesians 4:31:

> *"You shall not hate your brother in your heart, but you shall reason frankly with your neighbor, lest you incur sin because of him."*
> *Leviticus 19:17*
> *English Standard Version (ESV)*

> *Whoever says he is in the light and hates his brother is still in darkness. Whoever loves his brother abides in the light, and in him, there is no cause for stumbling. But whoever hates his brother is in the darkness and walks in the darkness, and does not know where he is going, because the darkness has blinded his eyes.*
> *1 John 2:9-11*
> *English Standard Version (ESV)*

> *Hatred stirs up strife, but love covers all offenses.*
> *Proverbs 10:12*
> *English Standard Version (ESV)*

> *Get rid of all bitterness, rage, and anger, brawling and slander, along with every form of malice.*
> *Ephesians 4:31*
> *New International Version (NIV)*

Hatred or hate is defined as:

> A deep and extreme emotional dislike, especially invoking feelings of anger or resentment. It

> can be directed against individuals, groups, entities, objects, behaviors, or ideas. Hatred is often associated with feelings of anger, disgust, and a disposition towards hostility. [32]
>
> In psychoanalysis, Sigmund Freud defined hate as an ego state that wishes to destroy the source of its unhappiness.[33]

When we feel extreme emotions of hatred quite often, it is a result of someone betraying, disappointing us, or we are holding on to resentment. When we hang on to emotions of hate, we are laying down the foundation for it to become an idol because hatred is in opposition to the word of God.

Often we use anger to protect or hide that we are hurt and may want to take revenge against the offender, thinking, "I didn't deserve that," but no matter what, we are not to hold on to hate. The Bible warns us in Leviticus 19:17 (see above) not to hate in order not to sin because of someone else bad behavior.

There could be medical consequences by holding onto hatred, especially over time, as the heart and

---

[32] https://en.m.wikipedia.org/wiki/Hatred
[33] Freud, S. (1915). The instincts and their vicissitudes

possible blood pressures can be effected; also, I've noticed that some people display anxiety and restlessness; therefore, it is time to let hatred go.

In 1 John 2 (see above), people that profess to be Christians and are not entirely obedient may say they live in the light. But if they do not love and have hatred in their heart toward other believers, they remain in darkness under the power of the corrupted sin nature. As God loves us, we are to love our brother (Christian brotherly love) and not be cruel but live in peace. According to Paul, "Because the darkness has blinded his eyes" refers to what he said in 1Corinthians 13: 2:

> *And if I have prophetic powers, and understand*
> *all mysteries and all knowledge, and if I*
> *have all faith, so as to remove mountains,*
> *but have not love, I am nothing.*
> *1 Corinthians 13:2*
> *English Standard Version (ESV)*

Fits of Rage

Fits of rage may be the result of holding on to anger or not being able to control one's temper; thus, it can be classified as an idol. In Proverbs 15:18, we read that a hot-tempered man stirs up strife while in Proverbs 14:29, one who is slow to anger has a great understanding, and in Proverbs 14:17 the scripture refers to a quick-tempered person as one that acts foolishly.

> *A hot-tempered man stirs up strife, but he who is slow to anger quiets contention.*
> *Proverbs 15:18 English Standard Version (ESV)*

> *Whoever is slow to anger has great understanding, but he who has a hasty temper exalts folly.*
> *Proverbs 14:29 English Standard" Version (ESV)*

> *A man of quick temper acts foolishly, and a man of evil devices is hated.*
> *Proverbs 14:17 English Standard Version (ESV)*

The definition of fit of rage according to Merriam-Webster:

> a: violent and uncontrolled anger
> b: a fit of violent wrath
> c: archaic: insanity[34]

The Scripture warns us against acts of rage and anger to protect us physically and emotionally. If not controlled over time, it can increase anxiety and high blood pressure. Like any other sin, people born with these symptoms of rage need

---

[34] https://www.merriam-webster.com/dictionary/rage

to learn to control them by admitting they have a problem and learning relaxation exercises, counseling, and prayer, asking God to break the chains of this sinful nature of anger.

Rage of anger comes when we are overwhelmed, wanting to explode because we do not have control of our feeling. One way to control anger is to change our attitude and think, is this worth getting angry over, and what will it accomplish? Perhaps it is time to walk away when we realize that life is short, and it cost more to be angry. We are not guaranteed tomorrow, so if we die, we would have wasted our time being angry.

A hasty temper person hurries to makes rash decisions just to make himself look like a fool. The foolish do not hold to the teachings of the Bible but take light and mock such teachings and consider sin as unimportant. Here is a saying about fools, "It is better to be thought a fool than to speak and remove all doubt." Proverbs 17:28 also reminds us of this:

> *Even fools are thought wise if they keep silent,*
> *and discerning if they hold their tongues.*
> Proverbs 17:28
> *New International Version (NIV)*

There are a wrong way and a right way of handling these fits. Unfortunately, people feel the need to fight and may lose self-control causing bodily harm while others may express themselves by punching a hole in the wall.

Here are examples of people displaying fits of anger:

> My friend's young son had a difficult time managing fits of anger, and once the young boy swung his fist with fits of rage, making contact with the door, and thus he punched a hole in it. Then another time, while playing with his punching bag, it bounced back and hit him on the head, so he got a large hat pin and stabbed it until he deflated the bag.

> A woman had run over her husband several times. She tried to kill him because she was overwhelmed with fits of rage over the husband having numerous affairs because she was a jealous wife, claiming she was trying to save her marriage. Unfortunately, divorce is part of our society more than ever, and it is so sad to see people ruin their lives because they cannot accept divorce, they foresee their future living with-

out their mate (their idol) or living alone.

When misunderstanding occurs, there is a right way to handle fits of rage, first calm down by taking deep breaths. Don't jump to conclusions but think about what the other person might have meant and ask, "What did they mean and what was their intention." Perhaps what they said wasn't what they meant, or their word was interpreted incorrectly.

It is better to surrender the possession of the rage and control it than allowing it to control us. One big concern other than letting it control lives is the effects it has on the heart. Here is an article regarding the impact of anger.

> "Two hours after an angry outburst, the chance of having a heart attack doubles," says Chris Aiken, MD, an instructor in clinical psychiatry at the Wake Forest University School of Medicine and director of the Mood Treatment Center in Winston-Salem, North Carolina.[35]

Since the brain is affected in times of rage, our thinking process may be hindered, so it is import-

---

[35] https://www.everydayhealth.com/news/ways-anger-ruining-your-health/

ant before making decisions to calm down by taking deep breaths or walking away. Once emotionally unattached to the situation, you can proceed in making sound decisions.

Factions and Envy

Faction and envy become an idol because of the intentions for breaking off into a small group to undermine the agenda of the whole group. It's usually to achieve a personal goal with selfish ambitions by not going along with the main plan or objectives of the group. Let's see what the Bible has to say about these two subjects in Acts 23:7, Jude 1:16-19, Galatians 5:19-21 and James 3:14-16:

> *And when he had said this, a dissension*
> *arose between the Pharisees and the*
> *Sadducees, and the assembly was divided.*
> *Acts 23:7*
> *English Standard Version (ESV)*

> *These are grumblers, malcontents, following*
> *their own sinful desires; they are loud-*
> *mouthed boasters, showing favoritism to*
> *gain advantage. But you must remember,*
> *beloved, the predictions of the apostles of our*
> *Lord Jesus Christ. They said to you, "In the*
> *last time there will be scoffers, following their*

*own ungodly passions." It is these who cause
divisions, worldly people, devoid of the Spirit.*
Jude 1:16-19
English Standard Version (ESV)

*Now the works of the flesh are evident:
sexual immorality, impurity, sensuality,
idolatry, sorcery, enmity, strife, jealousy,
fits of anger, rivalries, dissensions,
divisions, envy, drunkenness, orgies, and
things like these. I warn you, as I warned
you before, that those who do such things
will not inherit the kingdom of God.*
Galatians 5:19-21
English Standard Version (ESV)

*But if you harbor bitter envy and selfish
ambition in your hearts, do not boast
about it or deny the truth. Such "wisdom"
does not come down from heaven but is
earthly, unspiritual, demonic. For where
you have envy and selfish ambition, there
you find disorder and every evil practice.*
James 3:14-16
New International Version (NIV)

The definition of faction by Collins Dictionary:

Countable noun:

> A faction is an organized group
> of people within a large group,
> which opposes to some of the

ideas of the larger group and fights for its own idea[36]

Additional definition of faction by dictionary.com:

1. A feeling of discontent or covetousness with regard to another's advantages, success, possessions, etc.
2. An object of such feeling: Her intelligence made her the envy of her classmates.
3. Noun strong disagreement; a contention or quarrel; discord. difference in sentiment or opinion; disagreement.[37]

Definition of Envy by disctionary.com:

1. A feeling of discontent or covetousness with regard to another's advantages, success, possessions, etc.
2. An object of such feeling: Her intelligence made her the envy of her classmates.
3. Obsolete. ill will.[38]

Breaking off into a small group because of disagreements does not necessarily have to be a negative situation. For example, when someone sees a need that is not being met, and they are upset

---

[36] https://www.collinsdictionary.com/us/dictionary/english/faction

[37] https://www.dictionary.com/browse/dissension

[38] https://www.dictionary.com/browse/envy

TURN TO GOD FROM IDOLS

that others have not noticed, they may break off into a smaller group to rectify the problem. However, in this case, faction refers to people that break away because of dissensions they may have. These groups meet to undermine the intentions of the larger group to fulfill their own desires. Here is an example, there was a bookkeeper of a small church, and someone else in the group perceived that she was a better candidate for the job and wanted to be the bookkeeper. So she met with a small group to change the requirements of how long someone could hold the position as a bookkeeper. The idea was that the bookkeeper was to take a break and not allowed to have control of the books for a long time. This is a smart idea, and I recommend the books should be audited periodically. The term was changed, and at the end of the second year, the bookkeeper stepped down, which allowed the other person the opportunity to be the bookkeeper. Sadly, what she thought was a glamorous job turned out to be too much work, and she stepped down before the end of her term. Often this is the result of people who are jealous or envious of others' accomplishments, or they want the glory they perceive in others.

God gives us talents to be used for his glory. Some become the star, while others may be used in a different setting, yet in these cases, both are accomplishing the goal set by God. When we envy or are jealous of these people, we are questioning and saying that we do not believe that God sees and knows the big picture. God knows what we can handle, and therefore he allows some people to experience great achievements, such as valedictorian. In contrast, others that are shy and intimidated easily may not want to be at the forefront like a soloist or a lead singer. I have a saying I like to use, "God has a place for everyone," so instead of being afraid or envious, teach others and know God has a place and purpose for everyone.

Jealousy

Jealousy becomes an idol because it is self-centered, one may be envious of what others have, or accomplish. Also, jealousy makes people furious, which can make them dangerous if they proceed to avenge others. Scripture instructs us not to be jealous. Here are some verses that I choose regarding jealous behavior found in 1Corinthians 3:3, Job 5:2, Proverbs 6:34, and James 3:14-16:

> *For you are still of the flesh. For while there is jealousy and strife among you, are you not of the flesh and behaving only in a human way?*
> *1 Corinthians 3:3*
> *English Standard Version (ESV)*

TURN TO GOD FROM IDOLS

Surely vexation kills the fool, and
jealousy slays the simple.

Job 5:2
English Standard Version (ESV)

For jealousy makes a man furious, and he
will not spare when he takes revenge.
Proverbs 6:34
English Standard Version (ESV)

But if you have bitter jealousy and selfish
ambition in your hearts, do not boast
and be false to the truth. This is not the
wisdom that comes down from above, but
is earthly, unspiritual, demonic. For where
jealousy and selfish ambition exist, there
will be disorder and every vile practice.
James 3:14-16
English Standard Version (ESV)

Definition of jealous:

1. hostile toward a rival or one believed to enjoy an advantage envious of his success made his old friends jealous. They were jealous of his success.
2. intolerant of rivalry or unfaithfulness jealous of the slightest interference in household management—Havelock Ellis disposed to suspect rivalry or unfaithfulness, a jealous husband
3. vigilant in guarding a possession new colonies were jealous of their new inde-

pendence—Scott Buchanan— jealously adverb

Jealousy is an emotionally intense experience. Insecurity, fear, and envy are the results of one who feels a relationship is in danger since jealousy can involve a third person. When a person becomes jealous over an affair the spouse may have had and is unable to vent the anger, he can seek revenge by killing either the spouse, the third party, or even all three. Jealousy is not limited to just husbands and wives, fearing that one may be unfaithful, but it could be among siblings and friends. Often siblings want a relationship and the affection of their parents or family members because they do not want to be left out, so they become jealous. Jealousy can be the result of one perceiving that others have possessions or achieved goals they wish they had. Instead of being jealous of others, we are commanded to be thankful for what God has provided for us. We are not to compare ourselves to others but focus on God. Otherwise, we open ourselves to many types of temptations. God knows all our needs, and He gives generously as He will provide according to His will.

In times of divorce, though painful, but we do not have control of the situation, we should not be jealous over affairs that the spouse may have because when the spouse leaves to be with someone else, this could be a blessing and a time of personal growth. This is true, especially when people have a tendency of rage and anger and can easily lose their temper. God has used divorce to bring me closer to Him. Sometimes people have to be brought to the point of surrendering to look towards God for guidance in their life. Also, I believe that at times, God may allow divorce because He is protecting us from an unforeseen situation. After all, He knows the future.

Drunkenness

Drunkenness is an idol since this is the result of drinking too much, becoming intoxicated, and putting comfort in the liquor. The scriptures warn us to protect our hearts from carousing, drunkenness and the anxieties of life so that we do not die and thus lose our inheritance, the kingdom of God, see Luke 21:34-36, 1 Corinthians 6:10 and 1 Peter 4:3:

> *"Be careful, or your hearts will be weighed down with carousing, drunkenness and the anxieties of life, and that day will close on you suddenly like a trap. For it will come on all those who live on the face of the whole earth. Be always on the watch, and pray that you may be able to escape all that is about to happen and that you may be able to stand before the Son of Man."*
> *Luke 21:34-36*
> *New International Version (NIV)*

*Nor thieves, nor the greedy, nor
drunkards, nor revilers, nor swindlers
will inherit the kingdom of God.*
1 Corinthians 6:10
English Standard Version (ESV)

*For you have spent enough time in the past
doing what pagans choose to do – living
in debauchery, lust, drunkenness, orgies,
carousing and detestable idolatry.*
I Peter 4:3
New International Version (NIV)

The definition of Drunkenness by <u>vocabulary.com</u> is:

1. temporary state resulting from excessive consumption of alcohol
2. a dazed and staggering state caused by alcohol
3. stupefaction from drink
4. the act of drinking alcoholic beverages to excess
5. a long period of drinking consumption of alcoholic drinks
6. habitual intoxication; prolonged and excessive intake of alcoholic drinks leading to a breakdown in health and an addiction to alcohol such that abrupt deprivation leads to severe withdrawal symptoms[39]

---

[39] https://www.vocabulary.com/dictionary/drunkenness

TURN TO GOD FROM IDOLS

Drinking too much can be a result of cravings and the inability to control the desire to drink. People trying to forget their troubles turn to alcoholic beverages with the hope of washing away their blues. Moderately drinking alcoholic beverages can act as sedative affecting one's coordination. A drunkard may do something they otherwise would not do, expressing that they were too drunk and didn't know what they were doing. Binge drinking that is drinking excessively in a short period to have fun has unfortunately become socially accepted. Additionally, this leads to insufficient oxygen, so the person's skin can become clammy. Excessive drinking has taken the lives of many people due to fatal accidents and because of health issues affecting the liver and heart.

I've had the opportunity to volunteer at the Dream Center - Los Angeles, an organization that takes broken people to a community and addresses their immediate and long term needs; and in downtown Los Angeles' skid road. Opportunities include handing out backpacks filled with school supplies, clothing and shoes, and providing meals. Skid road is a deprived community, a place where the homeless and alcoholics live in rigged up shelters like tents. They have minimal personal belongings, and they do not have the means to provide for themselves nor their families. Drunkenness can also result in diseases, crime, and death. Scripture warns against such negative behavior as this can put a person in jeopardy of not inheriting the kingdom of God if they do not repent while they are still able.

Folly

When I think of folly, I think of foolish people lacking common sense with twisted values. These people can be oblivious of their surroundings as they are consumed with their thoughts and actions, see Proverbs 15:14 and Proverbs 15:21:

> *The heart of him who has understanding seeks knowledge, but the mouths of fools feed on folly.*
> *Proverbs 15:14*
> *English Standard Version (ESV)*

> *Folly is a joy to him who lacks sense, but a man of understanding walks straight ahead.*
> *Proverbs 15:21*
> *English Standard Version (ESV)*

The definition of folly is:

plural follies

1. lack of good sense or normal prudence and foresight his folly in thinking he could not be caught
2. a: criminally or tragically foolish actions or conduct

> b: obsolete: <u>evil</u>, <u>wickedness</u>; especially: lewd behavior
> 3. a foolish act or idea. The prank was a youthful folly
> 4. an excessively costly or unprofitable undertaking Paying so much for that land was folly since it was all rocks and scrub trees.
> 5. an often extravagant picturesque building erected to suit a fanciful taste[40]

Foolish people lack common sense or the inability to decipher what is acceptable, so they end up causing chaos by annoying others through an offensive lifestyle. These people tend to be impulsive and negligent because they do not foresee the potential danger they may cause. Most people will learn from their mistakes, but foolish people are repeated offenders.

Over the years, I have encouraged people to take advantage of offers made by employers, such as saving for their retirement by taking advantage of the 401k program. When the employee chooses to use the service, the company will match funds up to a certain percent. Since it's not a lot of money one has to set aside, and it's taken from their gross income, the employee may not miss it. So to me, it is foolish not to take advantage of this service as a

---

[40] https://www.merriam-webster.com/dictionary/folly

little for a long time can add up. We are reminded of this in Proverbs 13:11:

> *Wealth gained hastily will dwindle, but*
> *whoever gathers little by little will increase it.*
> *Proverbs 13:11*
> *English Standard Version (ESV)*

We are to live like there is no tomorrow, especially when opportunities arise to discuss the need for salvation to others. Time is short, and we should not be foolish but live each day with purpose. This is especially true when witnessing, encouraging, and teaching others about Jesus Christ as tomorrow is not guaranteed. Let's see what James 1:13-17 has to say about tomorrow:

> *Come now, you who say, "Today or tomorrow*
> *we will go into such and such a town and*
> *spend a year there and trade and make a*
> *profit" — yet you do not know what tomorrow*
> *will bring." What is your life? For you are*
> *a mist that appears for a little time and then*
> *vanishes. Instead, you ought to say, "If the*
> *Lord wills, we will live and do this or that."*
> *As it is, you boast in your arrogance. All such*
> *boasting is evil. So whoever knows the right*
> *thing to do and fails to do it, for him it is sin.*
> *James 4:13-17*
> *English Standard Version (ESV)*

I also tell people not to be foolish but to be cautious when surfing the internet. Attacking people

TURN TO GOD FROM IDOLS

on the computer through viruses has become a major issue resulting in people using unsecured websites. With the expansion of the medias' electronic forums, it has made it easy to track every movement one makes. Take caution when posting on popular social media sites, as it can be seen by thousands of people in a matter of minutes. When traveling don't post that you are away from home as thieves can see that you are not at home and rob you; they can be someone you know and least suspect. I say if you would be too embarrassed for your mom to see it, don't post it. The media can be a good way to communicate as it allows one to enjoy the pictures of family and friends living afar. This gives them an avenue to share; otherwise, one could miss out on milestones and achievements. However, be careful while using these applications as it is easy to fall into a false or foolish appearance habit making it appear that you have a perfect life with perfect children with halos.

The body is the temple of the Holy Spirit, and it is sad to see when people foolishly do not take care of themselves. I like to encourage people to not just sit in front of the TV all day long but to take walks for 30-45 minutes a day. Sadly, I have heard retirees say, "I am retired, and my job is to sit and watch TV all day." But as we get older, we can get stiff very easily by just sitting around doing nothing. You have heard the statement, "Use it or lose it" that also goes for the brain. Some illnesses are the result of poor eating, being idle, and a lack of exercise.

Lewdness

Lewdness is an abomination, wild inappropriate sexual behavior going against the word of God and becomes an idol since the total focus of these people is for personal satisfaction, see Jeremiah 13-27, Hosea 2:10 and Ezekiel 16:43.

> *Your adulteries and lustful neighings,*
> *your shameless prostitution! I have seen*
> *your detestable acts on the hills and*
> *in the fields. Woe to you, Jerusalem!*
> *How long will you be unclean?*
> Jeremiah 13:27
> *New International Version (NIV)*

> *So now I will expose her lewdness*
> *before the eyes of her lovers; no one*
> *will take her out of my hands.*
> Hosea 2:10
> *New International Version (NIV)*

> *Because you have not remembered the days*
> *of your youth, but have enraged me with all*
> *these things, therefore, behold, I have returned*
> *your deeds upon your head, declares the*

TURN TO GOD FROM IDOLS

Lord God. Have you not committed lewdness
in addition to all your abominations.
Ezekiel 16:43
English Standard Version (ESV)

Definition of lewd:

1. obsolete: evil, wicked
2. a. sexually unchaste or licentious, lewd behavior
   b. obscene, vulgar lewd remarks[41]

Definition of lewdness:

adjective, lewd·er, lewd·est.
1. Inclined to, characterized by, or inciting to lust or lechery; lascivious.
2. Obscene or indecent, as language or songs; salacious.
3. Obsolete.

- Low, ignorant, or vulgar.
- Base, vile, or wicked, especially of a person.
- Bad, worthless, or poor, especially of a thing.[42]

noun

The definition of lewdness is the quality of being very sexual

---

[41] https://www.merriam-webster.com/dictionary/lewd

[42] https://www.dictionary.com/browse/lewdness?s=t

> or lustful in an offensive way.
> An example of lewdness is asking people for sexual favors on the streets.[43]

A Lewd person is often classified as an offensive promiscuous prostitute, especially when hanging out with fleeting unstable people that are willing to jump into the net of destruction. This way of life does not only hurts the Lewd person physically and emotionally, but it can hurt their partners through diseases, especially in cases of Sexually Transmitted Diseases (STD).

Lewd does not only have to be an actor, but a vulgar person may make oral remarks that are obscene, offensive, and sexually inappropriate. The laws protecting public conduct of immoral and improper practices may vary by state. Some of the consequences may include incarceration, time in county jail, fines, probation, or community service.

In Hosea 2:10 (see above) - God threatened the idolatrous people, and they did not turn away from their evil ways. The leaders were prosperous and thought themselves to be wise, but when God stepped in, He brought them down in status, and thus they were despised by others. In Hosea 2:10, the idolatrous is referring to one that chose lovers,

---

[43] http://www.yourdictionary.com/lewdness

idols, and false gods over God. The scriptures use an uncommon term for lewdness that is not frequently used today, which is folly or foulness. God would expose the idolatrous' folly and punish her for not repenting, and therefore no one could save her from her punishment. Even though God had warned and put hindrance before them, they did not heed to His warning and repeatedly disobeyed Him, so He imposed His punishment. Since God's love is so deep, He will often use restraining grace, creating calamity to get our attention to repent. That is He will step back and allow us to do whatever we desire, but without restraining grace, we find that the sin can control us. In Hosea 2:10, God threatens them, but they continued to sin and not repent, and He punished them.

Sexual Immorality, Impurity, and Debauchery

The Scriptures are very precise and against living in a manner that is unholy and not pleasing to God, such as sexual immorality, impurity, and debauchery, which are sins of the heart and idols. We are instructed to reframe from wild parties where drinking and sexual sins are practiced because they can get out of control with scandalous activities. Sexual immorality is a sin against our own body, and such activities can cause many problems such as self-destruction and jealousy: Two scriptures to back this up are found in Proverbs 6:32a and Proverbs 6:34:

> *He who commits adultery lacks sense;*
> *he who does it destroys himself.*
> *Proverbs 6:32a*
> *English Standard Version (ESV).*

> *For jealousy makes a man furious, and he*
> *will not spare when he takes revenge.*
> *Proverbs 6:34*
> *English Standard Version (ESV)*

Since this is an abomination, I have included other Scriptures relating to Sexual Immorality, Impurity and Debauchery, Colossians 3:5, Mark 7:20-23, Romans 13:12-14, 1 Corinthians 5:1, Ephesians 5:18 and 1 Peter 4:3:

> *Put to death, therefore, whatever belongs to your*
> *earthly nature: sexual immorality, impurity,*
> *lust, evil desires, and greed, which is idolatry.*
> *Colossians 3:5*
> *New International Version (NIV)*

> *And he said, "What comes out of a person*
> *is what defiles him. For from within, out of*
> *the heart of man, come evil thoughts, sexual*
> *immorality, theft, murder, adultery, coveting,*
> *wickedness, deceit, sensuality, envy, slander,*
> *pride, foolishness. All these evil things come*
> *from within, and they defile a person."*
> *Mark 7:20-23*
> *English Standard Version (ESV)*

TURN TO GOD FROM IDOLS

The night is nearly over; the day is almost here. So let us put aside the deeds of darkness and put on the armor of light. Let us behave decently, as in the daytime, not in carousing and drunkenness, not in sexual immorality and debauchery, not in dissension and jealousy. Rather, clothe yourselves with the Lord Jesus Christ, and do not think about how to gratify the desires of the flesh.
Romans 13:12-14
New International Version (NIV)

It is reported commonly that there is fornication among you, and such fornication as it is not so much as named among the Gentiles, that one should have his father's wife.
1 Corinthians 5:1
King James Version (KJV)

Do not get drunk on wine, which leads to debauchery, instead, be filled with the Spirit.
Ephesians 5:18
English Standard Version (ESV)

For you have given time enough to the past to the doing of the things which the Gentiles delight in-pursuing, as you did, a course of habitual license, debauchery, hard-drinking, noisy revelry, drunkenness, and unholy image-worship.
1 Peter 4:3
English Standard Version (ESV)

Definition of Sexual Immorality:

> In the New Testament, the word most often translated "sexual immorality" is porneia. This word is also translated as "whoredom," "fornication," and "idolatry." It means "a surrendering of sexual purity," "purity," and it is primarily used of premarital sexual relations. From this Greek word, we get the English word pornography, stemming from the concept of "selling off." Sexual immorality is the "selling off" of sexual purity and involves any type of sexual expression outside the boundaries of a biblically defined marriage relationship.[44]

Definition of Impurity by Merriam Webster:

Plural impurities

1. something that is impure or makes something else impure removing impurities from water
2. the quality or state of being impure.

The definition of impure: not pure: such as:

a: lewd, unchaste

---

[44] https://www.gotquestions.org/sexual-immorality.html

b: containing something unclean:
foul, impure water
c: ritually unclean
d: mixed or impregnated with an extraneous and usually unwanted substance an impure chemical.[45]

Definition of debauchery by Merriam Webster:

> Extreme indulgence in bodily pleasures and especially sexual pleasures: behavior involving sex, drugs, alcohol, etc. that is often considered immoral[46]

While growing up, my mother instilled good moral value even though I was not a Christian. However, one of my friends and I went to a birthday party of a mutual friend. The party was pretty calm with everyone talking, drinking, and just having a good time. However, at the house, the owners had a room set aside where couples could go to have time alone. Now that could've been tempting and not appropriate, for most of the couples there were not married. I know some may say big deal as so many people wouldn't think twice of such activities. But remember that was a big deal especially back in the '70s and it should be a

---

[45] https://www.merriam-webster.com/dictionary/impure
[46] https://www.merriam-webster.com/dictionary/debauchery

big deal even today. If it was a sin, then it's still a sin today.

Sexual Immorality defined by Patheos:

> Sexual immorality is translated as fornication, sin against our own body. Fornication is defined as sexual intercourse between people not married to each other. Biblically, fornication has a little wider definition. It can refer to prostitution or promiscuous behavior or indulging in unlawful lust by either sex. It can also refer figuratively to committing idolatry.[47]

Impurity in terms of what the Scriptures refer to is someone who is contaminated sexually or of other sinful, immoral acts being corrupted into a sinful way.

Some may say a little impure thought can't hurt; however, it is destructive because it can mature into sin, affecting the entire body. Like many types of sin, we start with the tempting little things. We

---

[47] http://www.patheos.com/blogs/christiancrier/2014/08/18/what-is-the-bible-definition-and-explanation-of-fornication/

may think that these thoughts aren't going anywhere, that we have control, but over time this has been proven to be false. We give up peace and rest as we chase after something that can never satisfy our desires. The more we have, the more we want.

Debauchery is referred to as a continuous indulgence seeking lust and sexual pleasures while, "Partying" a term to describe immoral behavior by indulging in sex, drugs, and alcohol. I visually think of people partying as carousing and excessively drinking, dancing, celebrating, making merriment, sex, high spirits, cheer, and fun all night long. Debauchery is a lifestyle that God hates, and followers of Christ should not live this way as this can lead to destruction, lost from eternal salvation if one does not repent.

As we can see, these lifestyles lead to destruction and show a lack of wisdom. If you will note, this term, referring to immoral living is repeated throughout the Bible, and destruction is referring to the spiritual life, our soul. We are warned to be diligent and watch closely what we do and not to allow others to persuade or manipulate us to live a poisonous lifestyle. Peer pressure can bring fear as everyone wants to be liked, accepted, and want to fit in, which makes it difficult to say no. When people are persistent, then it is time to find new friends that will not entice you to follow in such a poor lifestyle.

Adultery and Lust

The Bible tells us that we should not lust, but everyone needs to take the responsibility not to entice or put out stumbling blocks that can cause others to fall spiritually. Lusting over another person can become our idol when we turn our focus onto the person. We should dress modestly and not be flirtatious as this can cause others to covet. My mother used to say if women who were promiscuous, stayed away, and not engage in such activities, then men would not have somewhere to go for their evil practices. I will take it a step further and say it is everyone's responsibility to behave in a Godly manner and not even look at another person with a lustful intent as stated in Exodus 20:14, 1 John 2:16 and Matthew 5:28:

> *You shall not commit adultery.*
> *Exodus 20:14*
> *New International Version (NIV)*

> *For everything in the world-the lust of the flesh, the lust of the eyes, and the pride of life comes not from the Father but from the world.*
> *1John 2:16*
> *New International Version (NIV)*

TURN TO GOD FROM IDOLS

> *But I say to you that everyone who looks at a woman with lustful intent has already committed adultery with her in his heart.*
> *Matthew 5:28*
> *English Standard Version (ESV)*

In 1 Corinthians 6:19-20, we learn that our body is a temple of the Holy Spirit, and in Psalms139:14-15, we were fearfully and wonderfully made. This is a reminder that we were created by God and are His precious children. In the Bible, the temple was built by experts using the finest of material such as gold, silver, and bronze that its beauty attracted people from all over, in the same way, God has made us fearfully and wonderful His masterpiece perfect according to His will. Therefore, we are called to not fall into temptation by abusing our bodies.

> *Or do you not know that your body is a temple of the Holy Spirit within you, whom you have from God? You are not your own, for you were bought with a price. So glorify God in your body.*
> *1 Corinthians 6:19-20*
> *English Standard Version (ESV)*

> *I praise you because I am fearfully and wonderfully made; your works are wonderful, I know that full well. My frame was not hidden from you when I*

> *was made in the secret place when I was*
> *woven together in the depths of the earth.*
> Psalm 139:14 -15
> *New International Version (NIV)*

Adultery Defined by Christian Bible Reference:

> In the Old Testament, adultery was understood as sexual relations between a married (or betrothed) woman and a man other than her husband. It was, therefore, a sin against the husband. In the New Testament, Jesus extended the definition of adultery to include sexual relations between a married man and a woman other than his wife (Mark 10:11-12, Luke 16:18). Other New Testament teachings also understand it that way (1 Corinthians 6:15-16, 1 Corinthians 7:2).[48]

The definition of adultery by Merriam Webster is:

> plural adulteries; voluntary sexual intercourse between a married person and someone other than that person's current

---

[48] Christian Bible reference site https://www.christianbiblereference.org/faq_adultery.htm

spouse or partner; also an act of adultery[49]

Lust defined by Wikipedia:

> The definition of Lust is a psychological force producing intense wanting for an object, or circumstance fulfilling the emotion. Lust can take any form, such as the lust for sexuality, money, or power. It can take such mundane forms as the lust for food as distinct from the need for food.[50]

We must be aware that lust comes from our mind as a lustful thought, and its progression continues from a mental picture and with technology into sexting leading to adultery. This does not happen overnight, but with time it can become a habit or addiction. With deliberate practices, we are not allowing nor trusting God to help us overcome the temptation to step away from such activities. We are to flee mentally, emotionally, and physically from lustful desires, as sin is still a sin. The levels of progression start with just a thought that something will make us happy or will be gratifying. Then we wait for an invitation or opportunity

---

[49] https://www.merriam-webster.com/dictionary/adultery
[50] Wikipedia https://en.m.wikipedia.org/wiki/Lust

to act out desire with the hope of achieving selfish pleasures. Therefore, we should commit to living righteously by deciding to live a good and moral life, by seeking first the Kingdom of God. Let's see how James 1:14-15 explains this thought:

> *But each person is tempted when they are dragged away by their own evil desire and enticed. Then, after desire has conceived, it gives birth to sin; and sin, when it is full-grown, gives birth to death.*
> *James 1:14-15*
> *New International Version (NIV)*

Evil Desires

Evil desires have been around from the beginning of time, as seen in Genesis 3:1-5. The serpent beguiled Eve with his cunning words by manipulating God's words to mislead her. Since Satan wants to be the ruler of the world, so he will still kill and destroy by lying in the hopes of leading people away from the true living God. We must be aware of Satan's schemes to deceive us by capitalizing on our weaknesses. The serpent played on Eve's weakness when the serpent said, "Did God really say, 'You must not eat from any tree in the garden'? and "You will not certainly die" "For God knows that when you eat from it your eyes will be opened, and you will be like God, knowing good and evil." When temptations or false teachings arise, we need to be prepared to fight with the best weapons. These weapons are with the help from God, Jesus, and the Holy Spirit by reading the Word of God and by prayer.

> *Now the serpent was more crafty than any of the wild animals the Lord God had made. He said to the woman, "Did God really say, 'You must not eat from any tree in the garden'? The woman said to the serpent, "We may eat fruit from the trees in the garden, but God did say, 'You must not eat fruit from the tree that is in the middle of the garden, and you must not touch it, or you will die.'" "You will not certainly die," the serpent said to the woman. "For God knows that when you eat from it, your eyes will be opened, and you will be like God, knowing good and evil."*
> *Genesis 3:1-5*
> *New International Version (NIV).*

The definition of evil desires by Life Ministry:

> We all have desires. Some of these desires are worthy, healthy, and should be pursued. Some of these desires are unworthy, deadly, and should be avoided. Other sexual desires are perverted and driven by evil. A desire is a strong feeling that drives us to attain or possess something which is, or we think

> is, within our reach. Evil is the absence of good, that which is sinful, vicious, corrupt, morally wrong, and wicked. So obviously, when you put together two words as powerful as evil and desire, there is a reaction that is doubly powerful.[51]

To determine whether a desire is good, we need to decide the intent for the desire. Does it go against the word of God, like a desire to covet your neighbor's wife, a desire to take revenge, and is this a self-centered venture? We start the process through our thoughts, because of our fallen nature, we follow through to evil practice desires. Once we give in to these evil desires, we are giving birth to sin, which can lead to death. But the scripture mandates us to put these evil desires behind us, put them to death. Colossians 3:5-6 includes evil desires in a list of behaviors, which are idolatry.

> *Put to death, therefore, whatever belongs to your*
> *earthly nature: sexual immorality, impurity,*
> *lust, evil desires, and greed, which is idolatry.*
> *Because of these, the wrath of God is coming.*
> *Colossians 3:5-6*
> *New International Version (NIV).*

---

[51] https://www.lifeministry.org/evil-desires

Evil desires also come from within our hearts and from the flesh because of our fallen human nature. This began with Eve in the garden. We are not to yield to sin but continually turn away. Satan tempts us through worldly desires. In Galatians 5:16 (see above), we are to walk by the Spirit and not fulfill the lust of the flesh. To put these evil desires to death, we need to take appropriate action of seeking God, reading of the Bible, and praying.

All desires are not evil such as a desire for a relationship with someone with mutual feelings, love, respect, self-control, faithfulness, recognition, or a desire to eat. Evil desire can be triggered by someone we pass along the road in a sexy outfit like a prostitute all dressed up, a good looking actor or songs about sex. This, in turn, begins the thought process with emotional feelings, which can eventually lead to action. We need to turn from evil desires by following the guidelines provided in the scripture, having faith, and believe in God through Jesus Christ. He alone can break these desires to honor God, stop compromising, start making good choices, and set our minds on things above.

Greed

Greed is idolatry, people seek to satisfy their desire to indulge in whatever makes them feel happy, good, or content, therefore, their idol is self. Greed appears quite often in both the Old and New Testament, here are a few scriptures taken from various books of the Bible which describes a greedy person behavior and consequences of greed.

> *The wicked borrows and does not pay back,*
> *but the righteous is generous and gives.*
> *Psalm 37:21*
> *English Standard Version (ESV)*

> *Wealth gained hastily will dwindle, but*
> *whoever gathers little by little will increase it.*
> *Proverbs 13:11*
> *English Standard Version (ESV)*

> *Whoever is greedy for unjust gain troubles his*
> *own household, but he who hates bribes will live.*
> *Proverbs 15:27*
> *English Standard Version (ESV)*

> *Then he said to them, "Watch out!*
> *Be on your guard against all kinds of*
> *greed; a man's life does not consist in*
> *the abundance of his possessions."*
> *Luke 12:15*
> *New International Version (NIV)*

TURN TO GOD FROM IDOLS

*Nor thieves, nor the greedy, nor
drunkards, nor revilers, nor swindlers
will inherit the kingdom of God.*
I Corinthians 6:10
English Standard Version (ESV)

*They are darkened in their understanding,
alienated from the life of God because of
the ignorance that is in them, due to their
hardness of heart. They have become callous
and have given themselves up to sensuality,
greedy to practice every kind of impurity.*
Ephesians 4:18-19
English Standard Version (ESV)

*Since an overseer is entrusted with God's
work, he must be blameless–not overbearing,
not quick-tempered, not given to drunkenness,
not violent, not pursuing dishonest gain.*
Titus 1:7
New International Version (NIV)

I have seen greedy people who are lazy and good actors at pretending they're working hard and give the appearance that they are very important by strutting around. Yes, I called these people good actors as they can fake their way. In reality, they let others do all the hard work to accomplish the set goals. Then, in the end, they will brag as to what a great job they had done. I knew someone who would do this, for example, The individual went to the fellowship hall, and to his surprise, the group was celebrating a twenty-fifth wedding anniversary for an active member of the group. When a friend of ours asked him about the preparation as she wanted to know who put together the event for the couple, at first, he had mentioned that he happened to be there at the right time as he was not aware that the group was going to celebrate the wedding anniversary. But when she further asked to give details of the preparations, he would say things like, "We received a contribution for the food, decorations, and entertainment, and we had the women prepare the food and decorate the hall." He took credit even though he was not there when the crew met to plan, setup, and execute the event.

Greedy people can be self-satisfying to the point that they can eat to their heart's content without regard to whether there is enough food for everyone. There was a friend that prepared a meal for her family and guest; however, the wife of the guest was delayed at work. The family and other guests decided to go ahead and eat, and after everybody, including the husband, finished eating, there was enough food left for his wife, but instead, the husband proceeded to eat the rest, requiring the friend to open a can of chicken noodle soup for the wife. Also, when eating out at a restaurant when the bill is laid on the table, they will slowly take out their wallet in the hope that someone else will pay the bill.

TURN TO GOD FROM IDOLS

Our society has played a big role in influencing us to want more and not be satisfied with what we have. An old saying I grew up with is, "We're trying to keep up with the Joneses (neighbor)." Wanting more has created a need for us to feed our egos with stuff, careers, accomplishments, and monetary gain. Often, we say we need something, but in reality, it is a want, become we are so accustomed to higher expectations that we allow greed to seep in. The scriptures instruct us to be generous, grateful, and content as God gives us all we need, love, joy, rest, peace, and He liberally provides. True contentment comes from Christ. 1 Timothy 6:6-11 is a good reference for this:

> *But godliness with contentment is great gain, for we brought nothing into the world, and we cannot take anything out of the world. But if we have food and clothing, with these we will be content. But those who desire to be rich fall into temptation, into a snare, into many senseless and harmful desires that plunge people into ruin and destruction. For the love of money is a root of all kinds of evils. It is through this craving that some have wandered away from the faith and pierced themselves with many pangs.*
> *1 Timothy 6:6-11*
> *English Standard Version (ESV).*

> *Whoever is greedy for unjust gain troubles his own household, but he who hates bribes will live.*
> *Proverbs 15:27*
> *English Standard Version (ESV)*

Orgies

While researching the word "orgy," I was surprised to see how it evolved. Therefore I have included one of my findings on its history. The English words "orgy" and "erotic" have their origins in Greek and ancient Greece, they were associated with mystery religions:

Orgy:

> While the concept of "orgy" today brings up images of unbridled sex, sexuality, and sexual intercourse, the origins of the word do not involve sex. Reaching far back in time, we see that "orgy" has its origins in the Indo-European root *werg- which means "to do." The English word "work" also comes from this stem.
>
> The Greek word "orgia," meaning "secret rites, worship," comes from the Indo-European *worg- which is a variation of *werg-. Among the Greeks, "orgia" was used in reference to the rites practiced in the worship of deities such as Orpheus and Dionysus. "Orgia" did not

describe sexual activity, though sex was a part of some of the ceremonies.

In ancient Greece, there were four basic kinds of religion: (1) the civic religion, (2) household religions, (3) philosophic religions, and (4) mystery religions. The "orgias" were a part of the mystery religions which were open only to initiates, unlike the public religions of this time and the private household religions. While sexuality and fertility were concerns, the primary goal of the "orgia" was to achieve an ecstatic union with the divinity.

"Orgia" passed into Latin and then into Old French, and finally landed in English in 1589 as "orgy" which was used to described the secret rites of the Greek and Roman religions. In the next few centuries, the religious meaning of the word disappeared and it now was used to describe sexual activities..[52]

---

[52] https://www.dailykos.com/stories/2013/5/25/1211622/
-Origins-of-English-Orgy-Erotic

The scriptures are clear and instruct that we are to walk properly during the day and night otherwise we will be in jeopardy of not inheriting the Kingdom of God if we do not stop these behaviors and repent, see Romans 13:13 and Galatians 5:21:

> Let us walk properly as in the daytime, not in orgies and drunkenness, not in sexual immorality and sensuality, not in quarreling and jealousy.
> *Romans 13:13*
> *English Standard Version (ESV)*

And envy; drunkenness, orgies, and the like. I warn you, as I did before, that those who live like this will not inherit the kingdom of God.
Galatians 5:21
New International Version (NIV)

The definition of Orgy is:

> noun, plural orgies.
> 1. Wild or drunken festivity or revelry, especially involving sex with multiple participants.
> 2. Any actions or proceedings marked by the unbridled indulgence of passions: an orgy of killing.
> 3. Orgies, (in ancient Greece) esoteric religious rituals, especially in the worship of Demeter or Dionysus, characterized in

later times by wild dancing, singing, and drinking.
4. Informal. a boisterous, rowdy party.[53]

When I first thought about this subject, orgies, I thought the Scriptures warns us against it, because God knew how devastating the consequences would be here on earth and especially for eternity. But why is it wrong? People may say, "Well, everyone else is doing it, so it must be okay." There are many benefits and reasons why God commands us to stay away from orgies or such sexual practices. God set the standards for our benefit as He intended marriage to be between a man and a woman, as seen in Genesis 1:27:

> *So God created mankind in his own*
> *image, in the image of God, he created*
> *them; male and female he created them.*
> Genesis 1:27
> New International Version (NIV)

Some of the dangers and consequences are venereal disease, sexually transmitted infections (STIs), or Sexual Transmitted Diseases (STD), which affect both partners and anyone else that they have had a sexual relationship with. Since diseases are often not discovered immediately, they can be fatal, especially when the cause is entangled from a previous illness that has not been medically treated.

---

[53] https://www.dictionary.com/browse/orgy

Other consequences can include emotional destruction. An unstable and weak person can feel worthless, shameful, and degraded, leading to depression or suicide.

Losing trust and respect among partners is another reason not to entertain such behavior. The partner will become suspicious whenever he goes out and perhaps thinks, "If he did this once, what will stop him from doing it again?" Our conscience is powerful and such events are hard to remove from the mind. Once trust is lost, it is difficult to regain as the partner may see the offender as someone who cannot be trusted and shut down to protect themselves for fear that it may happen again and making a fool out of them.

There aren't any lasting benefits; it ends up being a vice in which one continually searches for what makes them feel good. There is no satisfaction, but only a personal gratification for the moment that leads towards eternal death, as stated in Galatians 5: 21 (see above), one will not inherit the kingdom of God.

CHAPTER 6

Test the Lord

In the scriptures, we see that there are two views regarding testing the Lord. The two views are: when we are not to test God and when it is good to test the Lord.

1. *In Deuteronomy 6:16, Matthew 4:7, and Exodus 17:2, we are not to test God. Setting challenges for God can be an idol as we are not putting our faith or trust in God, as our thinking is rooted in doubt. Also, in testing God when we need a sign to believe, or we want God to prove Himself to us, that shows we lack in faith.*

> *Do not put the Lord your God to the test as you did at Massah.*
> *Deuteronomy 6:16*
> *New International Version (NIV)*

Jesus answered him, "It is also written: 'Do not put the Lord your God to the test.'"
Matthew 4:7
New International Version (NIV)

So they quarreled with Moses and said, "Give us water to drink." Moses replied, "Why do you quarrel with me? Why do you put the Lord to the test?"
Exodus 17:2
New International Version (NIV)

Luke 11:29, *asking for a sign displeases God.*

When the crowds were increasing, he began to say. "This generation is an evil generation. It seeks for a sign, but no sign will be given to it except the sign of Jonah."
Luke 11:29
English Standard Version (ESV)

Jonah is a book in the Old Testament recording the events of rebellions and then repentance of a man named Johan. The people of Nineveh were wicked, and Jonah was sent by God to prophesy the destruction of Nineveh. Instead, Jonah fled from the call of the Lord by embarking on a boat towards Tarshish. Because of his disobedience, the Lord caused a great wind on the sea, and a violent storm arose, so the ship he was on was threatened to break apart. When the men on the boat realized Jonah was the cause for the storm, they tossed him into the ocean, and he was swallowed by a giant fish. He was in the belly of the fish for three days and three nights. While in the fish, he cried for help and prayed to the Lord for forgiveness, so the Lord delivered him by causing the fish to vomit. This is a short story to show how the Lord forgives when everyone truly repents, Jonah asks God for forgiveness and repents and the Lord gave him a second chance.

In Matthew 4:7, the devil had taken Jesus up to the Holy City and stood on the highest point of the temple testing Jesus by telling Him to throw Himself down so that the angels would save Him from harm. The devils' purpose was to test Gods' word, and Jesus did not allow or fall into the devil's trap as Jesus honored God. That's why Jesus answered him:

> *Jesus answered him, "It is written: 'Do not put the Lord your God to the test.'"*
> *Matthew 4:7,*
> *New International Version (NIV).*

2. *In Malachi 3:10, we are to test the Lord when it pertains to tithing.*

Bring the whole tithe into the storehouse, that there may be food in my house. Test me in this," says the Lord Almighty, "and see if I will not throw open the floodgates of heaven and pour out so much blessing that there will not be room enough to store it.
Malachi 3:10
New International Version (NIV)

The definition of tithing per Bible Study Tools is:

> Tithe - a tenth of the produce of the earth consecrated and set apart for special purposes. The dedication of a tenth to God was recognized as a duty before the time of Moses. Abraham paid tithes to Melchizedek; and Jacob vowed unto the Lord and said, "Of all that thou shalt give me I will surely give the tenth unto thee."[54]

Tithing is the responsibility of all Christians, it is our duty to provide for the needs of the church regularly, and we are to do this with a cheerful heart. We are instructed in 1 Corinthians 16:1-2 to regular save from our earnings.

> *Now about the collection for the Lord's people:*
> *Do what I told the Galatian churches to do.*
> *On the first day of every week, each one of you*
> *should set aside a sum of money in keeping*
> *with your income. Saving it up, so that when*
> *I come, no collections will have to be made.*
> *1 Corinthians 16:1-2 New*
> *International Version (NIV).*

In my home church in Long Beach, California, there was a pastor that always said, "God loves a

---

[54] https://www.biblestudytools.com/dictionary/tithe/

cheerful giver," when it was time to pass the collection plate. This is a scriptural verse taken from 2 Corinthians 9:7:

> *Each of you should give what you have decided in your heart to give, not reluctantly or under compulsion, for God loves a cheerful giver.*
> *2 Corinthians 9:7*
> *New International Version (NIV).*

Tithing is an outward expression of our total surrender and obedience to God as we manage our finances following the directions found in the scriptures. God puts trust in His children to manage what He has provided, and it is not only to help the giver; it is meant to provide for the needs of the church and spreading the good news of Jesus. When people do not give tithe, it is because of the lies of ungodly beliefs and a desire for Satan to keep one in bondage. Malachi 3:9-10 says if one does not give tithe, they are under a curse because they are robbing God, but if one tithe, then it is a blessing:

> *You are under a curse–the whole nation of you–because you are robbing me. Bring the whole tithe into the storehouse, that there may be food in my house. Test me in this, says the Lord Almighty, "and see if I will not throw open the floodgates of heaven*

*and pour out so much blessing that there
will not be room enough to store it."*
*Malachi 3:9-10
New International Version (NIV)*

I was amazed at how the Lord provided a way for me to keep my house when I was going through a divorce. In those days, I received two paychecks per month, and one paycheck was not enough money to even cover the house payment. I had to learn to be frugal and be a wise steward of my income. One of my good friends told me about tithing as he said that God didn't need my help, but I needed God's help, so I began tithing. Promptly and with God's help, I was able to pay off my ex-husband, as I was to pay him for the equity that was due for him for his part of the investment in the house, and I was also able to pay the taxes and homeowner insurance. Also, God provided two strong Christians that helped me spiritually and emotionally:

1. Douglas Eugene Botts (now in heaven) was more like a spiritual dad as he helped me in understanding the Scriptures and was always there for me when my car broke down and whenever I needed minor assistance with the house.

    I have another story of God's grace upon my life. One day I was on my way to a bowling tournament, and my car made a loud sound, which scared me, so I stopped at a gas station and called Doug. When he asked my whereabouts in my excitement because I knew if one of us did not show up, the team would have to forfeit the match, I hurriedly gave him the name of two streets that ran parallel. This was before cell phones, so he could not call me back for clarification. Somehow, he figured out the path I would have taken to my destination, and he found me. He hurriedly took out a part that was used with the air conditioner and told me to go on.

2. The other person was Mrs. Hariklia "Rickie" Radoumis (now in heaven), who was like a Christian mom to me. Bless her heart; I could have called her every day as she always had time for me with her kind words and loving guidance. She naturally held firmly to the word of God, and at a time, my world was darkest, she drew me to the source of her light, Jesus.

I'm so thankful that though I had to go through this horrible experience, I can see the hand of God in my everyday life. I keep my eyes on the Lord and remember what he has done in the past and what he's doing even today. He does this because He loves us unconditionally and wants to help with our daily needs.

CHAPTER 7

Man's Rules

Traditions

When I think of tradition, the first thing that comes to my mind is the movie *Fiddler on the Roof*. I think of the influence put on the dad to allow his daughters to marry for love instead following the tradition, which required the dad to select husbands for his daughters. Keeping with tradition was such a challenge because of the unrest for the Jewish people in 1905, according to this story.

In 2 Thessalonians 2:15, the writer (some people question whether it was Paul the Apostle or not) instructs Christians to stand firm holding onto traditions handed down by the apostles as God directed. In Colossians 2:8, we are to be cautious not to be trapped with false worldly teachings. In Mark 7:3-9, Jesus was answering the Pharisees and the scribes because the disciples did not follow their traditions. Jesus told the Pharisees and the scribes that they were putting their traditions above the commandment of God as their hearts were far from God.

> *So then, brothers, stand firm and hold to the traditions that were taught by us, either by our spoken word or by our letter.*
> *2 Thessalonians 2:15*
> *English Standard Version (ESV)*

> *See to it that no one takes you captive by philosophy and empty deceit, according to human tradition, according to the elemental spirits of the world, and not according to Christ.*
> *Colossians 2:8*
> *English Standard Version (ESV)*

> *(For the Pharisees and all the Jews do not eat unless they wash their hands properly, holding to the tradition of the elders, and when they come from the marketplace, they do not eat unless they wash. And there are many other traditions that they observe, such as the washing of cups and pots and copper vessels and dining couches.) And the Pharisees and the scribes asked him, "Why do your disciples not walk according to the tradition of the elders, but eat with defiled hands?" And he said to them, "Well did Isaiah prophesy of you hypocrites, as it is written, "'This people honors me with their lips, but their heart is far from me; in vain do they worship me, teaching*

> *as doctrines the commandments of men.' You leave the commandment of God and hold to the tradition of men." And he said to them, "You have a fine way of rejecting the commandment of God in order to establish your tradition!"*
> Mark 7:3-9
> *English Standard Version (ESV)*

The definition of traditions:

noun
1. The handing down of statements, beliefs, legends, customs, information, etc., from generation to generation, especially by word of mouth or by practice: a story that has come down to us by popular tradition.
2. Something that is handed down: the traditions of the Eskimos.
3. A long-established or inherited way of thinking or acting[55]

In Matthew 23:23, Jesus condemns the Pharisees not for what they did but for neglecting the more important matters of the law of justice, mercy, and faithfulness. This is because the Pharisees put a higher value on their own rules/laws by enforcing rules that no one could successfully achieve, not even themselves. Thus, they made their laws and traditions into an idol by putting their law above

---

[55] https://www.dictionary.com/browse/tradition

the law of God. The Pharisees held themselves in high esteem and drew attention to themselves as one with high religious authority seeking recognition in the community.

> *Woe to you, teachers of the law and Pharisees, you hypocrites! You give a tenth of your spices — mint, dill, and cumin. But you have neglected the more important matters of the law — justice, mercy, and faithfulness. You should have practiced the latter, without neglecting the former.*
> Matthew 23: 23
> New International Version (NIV)

Colossians 2:8 (see above) is a good reminder to be alert for many views that are being expressed in the media that can sway our opinion from the truths of the Bible. They practice deceit with misguided teaching according to human traditions by not holding fast to the teachings found in the scriptures.

Some churches sway away from the traditions of God when they water down scriptures to appease their congregation as dictated by the changing moral values and thinking of the culture. They use their beliefs as a means to make people feel loved, comfortable, and part of a family without depending on the true living God or they don't acknowledge Jesus as their Messiah, Savior. They turn their beliefs to a more broadminded god who accepts a different lifestyle. Or some churches may turn away from their beliefs as they may say God has given them a new revelation.

Following rules to continue in the traditions of leaders and family reminds me of a story about someone following the tradition he grew up with, even though he did not agree with it. A friend and I were speaking to a gentleman and when he was asked if he believed in what his church preached he said he did not agree with them, but he said this is what he did growing up so even if he did not agree with the church, he felt he needed to continue going. As individuals, we are responsible for making the right choices and why it is important to understand the teaching of the Bible. The only way to eternal salvation is by individually accepting Jesus Christ as our personal savior; this is a gift. He has paid the price for us through His death on the cross. When I was a new Christian, someone said, "God doesn't have grandchildren because it is a choice all of us individually have to make."

In some of these cases, God, Jesus Christ, and the Holy Spirit are eliminated from their beliefs, and thus they worship gods made by man or someone they have elevated to be their god.

CHAPTER 8

Foreigners

Temporary Home - World

Thinking about how the world can become an idol seemed interesting to me, especially since God created the world and everything in it. Then I was reminded what it said in 1 John 2:16, that not all things come from God but comes from the flesh, such as lust and pride. Romans 12:2 instructs us not to be conformed to the patterns of the world and not love the world more than we love God. See 1 John 2:15.

> *For everything in the world – the lust of the flesh, the lust of the eyes, and the pride of life – comes not from the Father but from the world. The world and its desires pass away, but whoever does the will of God lives forever.*
> *1 John 2:16,*
> *New International Version (NIV).*

TURN TO GOD FROM IDOLS

*Do not conform to the pattern of this
world, but be transformed by the renewing
of your mind. Then you will be able to
test and approve what God's will is —
his good, pleasing, and perfect will.*
Romans 12:2
New International Version (NIV)

*Do not love the world or anything in
the world. If anyone loves the world,
love for the Father is not in them.*
1 John 2:15
New International Version (NIV)

Definition of world:

1. a: the earthly state of human existence
   b: life after death — used with a qualifier the next world
2. the earth with its inhabitants and all things upon it[56]

We are commanded not to love the world or anything in the world over our love of God. Our main vision should be on the journey that leads to our forever home, eternal salvation, by keeping our focus on living in righteousness. Our existence for a meaningful life should be enfolded with the presence of God as we fellowship with Him and proclaim His teachings. Proclaiming the Gospel of Jesus Christ to those around us so they can join

---

[56] https://www.merriam-webster.com/dictionary/world

us in the celebration when we get to heaven. In Mark 16:15, we see the command that Jesus gave to preach the gospel:

> *He said to them, "Go into all the world*
> *and preach the gospel to all creation."*
> Mark 16:15
> *New International Version (NIV)*

But when we are working and striving to achieve goals, our focus is not always directed in being a servant of God as Jesus taught. When overwhelmed with life's many demands, we need to stop, meditate, read the Bible, pray, and seek the Lord for His guidance. God's Word is true, and we can count on Him in every situation of life, whether in times of poverty or wealth and sickness or health.

While living in California, I was approached by two elderly women that stated how bored they were so they would go to the market just to have something to do. Also, I remember when I was working, I used to joke around and say, "I want a job where I can put my feet on top of the desk and eat Bon Bon's all day long" now that would have been boring and depressing. However, this is a time to enjoy life by serving others as the Lord Jesus was the best example we have, as seen in Philippians 2:7:

TURN TO GOD FROM IDOLS

> *Rather, he made himself nothing by*
> *taking the very nature of a servant,*
> *being made in human likeness.*
> *Philippians 2:7*
> *New International Version (NIV)*

There are so many opportunities, such as visiting the shut-in and those in hospitals, helping the widows or widowers, providing meals for the homeless or shut-ins, working with the youth, providing for those less fortunate, and the list goes on. Matthew 25:34-40 is a good place to see what the Lord has to say about this:

> *Then the King will say to those on his right,*
> *'Come, you who are blessed by my Father,*
> *inherit the kingdom prepared for you from the*
> *foundation of the world. For I was hungry, and*
> *you gave me food, I was thirsty, and you gave*
> *me drink, I was a stranger, and you welcomed*
> *me, I was naked, and you clothed me, I was*
> *sick, and you visited me, I was in prison,*
> *and you came to me.' Then the righteous will*
> *answer him, saying, 'Lord, when did we see*
> *you hungry and feed you, or thirsty and give*
> *you drink? And when did we see you a stranger*
> *and welcome you, or naked and clothe you?*
> *And when did we see you sick or in prison and*
> *visit you?' And the King will answer them,*
> *'Truly, I say to you, as you did it to one of the*
> *least of these my brothers, you did it to me.'*
> *Matthew 25:34-40*
> *English Standard Version (ESV)*

Many new Christians that I have met are so excited about learning of the saving grace of Jesus Christ that their enthusiasm can be contagious like in the story of the Samaritan woman, I love her enthusiasm. In John 4:19, 29-30, Jesus was able to tell her all about her life, and she was amazed and did not stop there as she went back to her town to let everyone know about the man she met. Here is her response to Jesus:

> *"Sir," the woman said, "I can see that you are a prophet." but she did not stop there she went back to her town and told the people 29 "Come, see a man who told me everything I ever did. Could this be the Messiah?" They came out of the town and made their way toward him.*
> *John 4:19, 29-30*
> *New International Version (NIV)*

Like the Samaritan woman, all of us can go out and proclaim the message of Jesus Christ. Jesus preached the word of God and lived out His life accordingly. Death was not the end because even though He was buried, on the third day, He arose. He did this in obedience to His Father so that we can have the assurance of eternal salvation. Wouldn't it be wonderful if all our family members and friends were all saved, and we knew that someday we would see them in heaven? The purpose of this temporary home is to live in obedience to the teachings of the word of God and witness to all. There are many ways one can communicate the good news to others, such as through preaching, music, and being a good example.

We may not have opportunities to witness others orally, but we can be a witness through our actions by living a Godly life. People may see your peaceful spirit and may wonder how can you be so calm even in difficult times. Before I became a Christian, I met a woman that seemed to be too happy, and I thought, "Is she for real." She always had a big smile and an encouraging word, even while going through hard times. She was able to do this because of her relationship with God, and she kept a positive attitude. I learned later that she was a Christian and lived with peace in her heart as she pursued a life of righteousness. This is a way to open the door for others to inquire and search for the hope you may display. I've heard people say, "You better be careful of what you say or do; people are watching you." Christians especially can be scrutinized as they are expected to live a perfect life, but the reality is Christians are human beings and make mistakes too. The difference is that Christians sin, then repent and strive to live in righteousness.

CHAPTER 9

Stars, Astrology, Fortune telling and Horoscopes

People often rely on fortunetellers, horoscopes, palm readings, looking into a crystal ball, and other spiritual mediums. They seek answers, help, and advice regarding their future, personal affairs, careers, and for such things as financial or family issues. These mediums are not new today, and some people may believe that God's creation, like stars, may be powerful, but it is not the created object that has the power but the creator, God. People read the horoscopes and believe in them because they want to know about the future, even if it is only for the day. If someone reads their horoscopes daily, over time, something is bound to come true just because it is statistically possible. Fortunetellers were popular for a time with some of my friends, but I never saw any true lasting results. This just gave them false hope. Predictions that fortunetellers make are not consistent even within themselves, I've heard it is unpredictable, a 50/50 percent chance.

Yet the scriptures reveal the future; just look at The Old Testament, which predicted the future, and in the New Testament, we have seen and are seeing as the future unfold. In Daniel 2:27-28, the magicians, enchanters, sorcerers, astrologers, and the wise men of Babylon were unable to interpret the king's dream. Daniel was aware of the importance of prayer, so he prayed for wisdom to be able to interpret the dream as he knew only God could give him the meaning. When we pray, we are in communication and fellowship with God. God knows our heart, but our prayer is to show our reliance and need for His help and to obtain wisdom. After all, God is omniscient and already knows what we need. Let's take a look at Psalms 139:4:

> *Daniel answered the king and said, "No wise man, enchanter, magician or astrologers can show to the king the mystery that the king has asked, but there is a God in heaven who reveals mysteries, and he has made known to King Nebuchadnezzar what will be in latter days."*
> *Daniel 2:27-28*
> *English Standard Version (ESV)*

> *Before a word is on my tongue, you,*
> *Lord, know it completely.*
> *Psalms 139:4*
> *New International Version (NIV).*

Praying helps us move toward God so that we can receive His blessings by being submissive and sincere. Philippians 4:6 reminds us not to be anxious but present our requests to God.

> *Do not be anxious about anything, but in*
> *every situation, by prayer and petition, with*
> *thanksgiving, present your requests to God.*
> *Philippians 4:6*
> *New International Version (NIV)*

Naturalism

Naturalism is a belief by atheists that the world was evolved and not created by God, and they are trying to prove it scientifically. However, we know this is incorrect as there is evidence everywhere that suggests and proves that God is the creator. Genesis 1:1 says God is the creator. Also, see Psalms 14:1 about those that say there is no God:

> *In the beginning, God created*
> *the heavens and the earth.*
> *Genesis 1:1*
> *New International Version (NIV)*

TURN TO GOD FROM IDOLS

The fool says in his heart, "There is no God." They are corrupt, they do abominable deeds; there is none who does good.
Psalms 14:1
English Standard Version (ESV)

The definition of Naturalism by Vocabulary.com:

Is the belief that nothing exists beyond the natural world. Instead of using supernatural or spiritual explanations, naturalism focuses on explanations that come from the laws of nature. Also:

1. n An artistic movement in the 19th century France; artists and writers strove for detailed realism and factual description.
2. n (philosophy) the doctrine that the world can be understood in scientific terms without recourse to a spiritual or supernatural explanation.[57]

Naturalism believes that there are no supernatural or spiritual laws that operate the world, but there is only physical and material matter. They believe there is no soul and no creator; therefore, our senses like pleasure, pain, health, and self are merely a physical reaction.

Compelling Truth explains Broad Naturalism as:

---

[57] https://www.vocabulary.com/dictionary/naturalism

> Broad Naturalism - Broad naturalists
> also deny God and the human soul, but
> they admit that consciousness, thought,
> and value (both in preferences and
> morality) do exist. Such things do not
> belong in the spiritual realm; instead,
> they are emergent physical states
> of extremely complex neurology. In
> response to the horrifying consideration
> that every action is pre-determined,
> broad naturalists rely on evolution.[58]

They believe that though they are not able to explain or prove evolution, it is a matter of further research. The good news is that there is enough evidence that life came with the aid of an outside source, God, as seen in Genesis 1:1 (see above).

Naturalists are avid environmentalists and are big in saving the world through what is known as the "Think Green" idea.

THINK GREEN

> Because of this total focus on the world,
> naturalists are avid environmentalists. From
> the smallest private acts of consideration
> like not littering to the largest issues of social
> accountability like corporate prevention of
> pollution, they challenge all of us to protect our

---

[58] https://www.compellingtruth.org/what-is-naturalism.html

planet. The environmental drive is a diverse scientific, social, and political movement for addressing environmental or "green" issues. Within most of the major religions of the world—including Christian, Hindu, Muslim, and Buddhist—are "green" proponents bent on saving the world. Taking care of our ecosystem transcends all national and spiritual borders. Some believe if we all pull together in this higher cause, the world will become not only a healthier place to live but also a more harmonious and united family.[59]

Taking care of this temporary home is a good idea; we should all take responsibility because God is the creator, and He created everything good for our use. 1Timothy 4 reminds us:

> *For everything God created is good,*
> *and nothing is to be rejected if it is*
> *received with thanksgiving.*
> 1Timothy 4:4
> *New International Version (NIV).*

God creates, controls, protects, and determine when we will take our final breath. When I was a child, we traveled to Mexico to visit dad's mom and family, and while we were there, we were to sing to them. One of the songs that we sang was,

---

[59] https://findanswers4life.wordpress.com/2015/10/14/naturalism/

"He's got the whole world in His hands," and isn't this true the Creator has our fate, and the fate of the world is in His hands.

CHAPTER 10

Warning

The Bible has many scriptures that warn us against following any type of idol so that we do not turn from God, our faith, or Jesus. Here are four verses that warn us of the consequences if we turn towards other gods, they are found in Psalm 16:4, Leviticus 20:6, 1 Chronicle 10:13-14 and Deuteronomy 18:9-13:

> *Those who run after other gods will suffer more and more. I will not pour out liberation of blood to such gods or take up their names on my lips.*
> *Psalm 16:4*
> *New International Version (NIV)*

> *If a person turns to mediums and necromancers, whoring after them, I will set my face against that person and will cut him off from among his people.*
> *Leviticus 20:6*
> *English standard version (ESV)*

> *So Saul died for his trespass which he committed against the Lord, because of the word of the Lord which he did not keep; and also because he asked counsel of a medium, making inquiry of it, and did not inquire of the Lord. Therefore He killed him and turned the kingdom to David, the son of Jesse.*
> 1 Chronicles 10:13-14
> New American Standard Bible(NASB)

> *When you enter the land, the Lord, your God, is giving you, do not learn to imitate the detestable ways of the nations there. Let no one be found among you who sacrifices their son or daughter in the fire, who practices divination or sorcery, interprets omens, engages in witchcraft, or casts spells, or who is a medium or spiritist or who consults the dead. Anyone who does these things is detestable to the Lord; because of these same detestable practices, the Lord your God will drive out those nations before you. You must be blameless before the Lord your God.*
> Deuteronomy 18:9-13
> New International Version (NIV)

Words of Caution and Warnings:

- Interrupting someone who is speaking does not give them the respect they deserve, instead, listen and not be quick to speak. This frustrates me when I interrupt others because often, I want to say something before I forget. If it is important, I am sure the Holy Spirit will bring it to remembrance. James 1:19-21 reminds us to be quick to hear and slow to speak:

Know this, my beloved brothers: let every
person be quick to hear, slow to speak, slow to
anger; for the anger of man does not produce
the righteousness of God. Therefore put
away all filthiness and rampant wickedness
and receive with meekness the implanted
word, which is able to save your souls.
James 1:19-21
English Standard Version (ESV)

- When we speak, we are to choose our words wisely, making sure we are keeping away from filthiness and ungodly speaking. Crude jokes are not acceptable, but instead, we should speak words that are uplifting to encourage others. From time to time, we all need words of encouragement because people may come with heartaches or grief causing them much pain. Therefore, we need not to react harshly but be patient. Here are some verses regarding filthiness and encouragement, see Ephesians 5:4, Ephesians 4:29 and Proverbs 15:4:

Let there be no filthiness nor foolish talk
nor crude joking, which are out of place,
but instead let there be thanksgiving.
Ephesians 5:4
English Standard Version (ESV)

> *Let no corrupting talk come out of your mouths, but only such as is good for building up, as fits the occasion, that it may give grace to those who hear.*
> *Ephesians 4:29*
> *English Standard Version (ESV)*

> *A gentle tongue is a tree of life, but perverseness in it breaks the spirit.*
> *Proverbs 15:4*
> *English Standard Version (ESV)*

- In the Scriptures, we are warned to walk away from temptation as it is easy to be misled by them. Couples live in sin if there are practicing sex out of marriage. Sadly, people make excuses as to why it is okay even though they may know right from wrong. Some excuses I have heard are: God understands my situation, I'm too lonely, or I am afraid to live alone, and after all, everyone is doing it. But we must stop and see what the Bible says about this and not go against the word of God. As Christian, we need to take our guidance from the word of God as sin is still sin; just because everyone else is doing it doesn't make it right.

- We are warned and commanded not to bow down to idols and worship anyone or anything but God. Here are a few more verses to remind us what the Bible has instructed. See Exodus 20:5, Leviticus 26:1-2, 2 Kings 17:35, and Joshua 23:16 :

You shall not bow down to them or serve them,
for I the Lord your God am a jealous God.
Exodus 20:5
English Standard Version (ESV)

You shall not make idols for yourselves or
erect an image or pillar, and you shall not
set up a figured stone in your land to bow
down to it, for I am the Lord your God.
Leviticus 26:1-2
English Standard Version (ESV)

The Lord made a covenant with them
and commanded them, "You shall not
fear other gods or bow yourselves to them
or serve them or sacrifice to them."
2 Kings 17:35
English Standard Version (ESV)

If you transgress the covenant of the Lord
your God, which he commanded you, and go
and serve other gods and bow down to them.
Then the anger of the Lord will be kindled
against you, and you shall perish quickly from
off the good land that he has given to you.
Joshua 23:16
English Standard Version (ESV)

And they abandoned the Lord, the God of
their fathers, who had brought them out of

> *the land of Egypt. They went after other*
> *gods, from among the gods of the peoples*
> *who were around them, and bowed down to*
> *them. And they provoked the Lord to anger.*
> *Judges 2:12*
> *English Standard Version (ESV)*

- Also, be aware of false teachings. This has become a big issue with many people openly expressing their opinions. According to Tim Challies' blog in *The Five Tests of False Doctrine,* he states that several known preachers have misinterpreted the Scriptures.[60] It is our responsibility to verify doctrines for its validity, making sure its origin is according to the word of God and not by man. Here are verses regarding testing the spirit, see 1 John 4:1 and 1 Thessalonians 5:21:

> *Beloved, do not believe every spirit*
> *but test the spirits to see whether they*
> *are from God, for many false prophets*
> *have gone out into the world.*
> *1 John 4:1*
> *English Standard Version (ESV)*

> *But test everything; hold fast what is good.*
> *1 Thessalonians 5:21*
> *English Standard Version (ESV)*

---

[60] https://www.challies.com/articles/test-every-doctrine-test-every-teacher/

CHAPTER 11

Spiritual Fullness in Christ

Living in spiritual fullness in Jesus Christ begins with the acceptance of Jesus Christ as your Personal Savior. This journey continues as a solid foundation is set through the reading of the Word, praying, and worshiping with other believers. Colossians 2:6-9 reminds us to beware of false teachings so that we will not be swayed away from the true word of the gospel of Jesus Christ.

> *So then, just as you received Christ Jesus as Lord, continue to live your lives in him, rooted and built up in him, strengthened in the faith as you were taught, and overflowing with thankfulness. See to it that no one takes you captive through hollow and deceptive philosophy, which depends on human tradition and the elemental spiritual forces of this world rather than on Christ. For in Christ, all the*

> *fullness of the Deity lives in bodily form, and*
> *in Christ, you have been brought to fullness.*
> *He is the head over every power and authority.*
> Colossians 2:6-9
> New International Version (NIV)

Our affections and loyalty should be to God by seeking the things above in holiness. We are to follow the teachings commanded by God and not those made up by man, especially those that go against the word of God. Jesus is the best example of what God desires from us as He demonstrated His obedience by dying on the cross. Jesus lived a holy and sinless life as He wanted to please his Father in everything He did, and He did it with love. Therefore, we should follow the teachings found in Colossians 3:12-14:

> *Therefore, as God's chosen people, holy*
> *and dearly loved, clothe yourselves with*
> *compassion, kindness, humility, gentleness,*
> *and patience. Bear with each other and forgive*
> *one another if any of you has a grievance*
> *against someone. Forgive as the Lord forgave*
> *you. And over all these virtues put on love,*
> *which binds them all together in perfect unity.*
> Colossians 3:12-14
> New International Version (NIV)

CHAPTER 12

Conclusion

God's desire is for His children to live an abundant life with peace in their hearts, but more importantly, He wants fellowship with His children now and for eternity. No matter which idol one worships and bows down to, one will miss out on God's best for their life. The result will be the separation from the one true loving God. The good news is that God forgives those that repent. Now is the time to repent and strive to live a Godly life before it is too late.

Years ago, I found myself in the hospital and was possibly in need of a blood transfusion. However, the doctor informed me that he would not give me a blood transfusion, even though I had lost half of my blood. He said that even 1% of tainted blood was not good, and he did not want to take a chance of putting my life in danger of any other medical problems. Then one day, I was asked, "How do we know if heaven and hell are real"? My first answer is we believe by faith because we read it in the word of God. However, taking into account what the doctor said, I asked them, "What if there is only a 1% chance that this is true?" Would you want to live for eternity in heaven or hell? I heard a saying that went something like this, "I'd rather live my life as a Christian and find out I was wrong than to live as a non-Christian and find out Christianity was true" (And I believe the word of God is true). Don't take the chance; don't gamble with your life; it is too precious, and eternity is a long time. I pray when we take our last breath here on earth, we will meet in heaven.

If you want to know how to live an abundant life, full of meaning, joy, holy and acceptable to God, you must:

- Admit that you are a sinner and have sinned
- Repent, ask God to forgive you
- Turn from your old sinful ways and turn to God
- Confess that Jesus Christ is your personal Savior and lord

Romans 10:9-13 gives more details to the process of salvation. Matthew 18:14 reminds us that God loves you and does not want you to perish. Ephesians 3:20 God can help in any situation; just ask knowing that He will answer you and then give Him thanks.

> *If you declare with your mouth, "Jesus is Lord," and believe in your heart that God raised him from the dead, you will be saved. For it is with your heart that you believe and are justified, and it is with your mouth that you profess your faith and are saved. As Scripture says, "Anyone who believes in him will never be put to shame." For there is no difference between Jew and Gentile – the same Lord is Lord of all and richly blesses all who call on him, for, "Everyone who calls on the name of the Lord will be saved."*
> *Romans 10:9-13*
> *New International Version (NIV)*

> *In the same way, your Father in heaven is not willing that any of these little ones should perish.*
> *Matthew 18:14*
> *New international Version (NIV)*

> *Now to him who is able to do far more than all we ask or think, according to his power at work within us, to him be glory to the Church and in Christ Jesus throughout all generations, forever and ever Amen."*
> *Ephesians 3:20*
> *English Standard Version (ESV)*

When I began to write this book, I felt the Lord is leading me to write about what was important and in my heart. It saddens me to see people worshiping idols. In my life, I have reasoned why something was okay just to find out that God was nudging me and trying to direct me on the right path. God speaks to us in our hearts, but because we are stubborn and think we are smart, we do not heed towards truth. We can reason and interpret the word to easily accommodate our wishes, but in our hearts, we know it is still wrong. Keep in mind God does not look for perfection, but we are to mature spiritually so that He can use us to build His kingdom. If a religion teaches that it is okay to worship anyone other than God, Jesus Christ, our Lord, then know that as a Christian (Christ-follower), it is an idol.

CHAPTER 13

Final Note from the Author

As I look back at my life, even before I understood about God, I can see how God has shown mercy (a blessing that is an act of divine favor or compassion)[61], and given me grace (Grace can be variously defined as "God's favor toward the unworthy" or "God's benevolence on the undeserving." In His grace, God is willing to forgive us and bless us abundantly, even though we don't deserve to be treated so well or dealt with so generously.)[62]. He protects His children as it was evident during a time of unrest while living in Los Angeles, California. Saying this does not mean my life has been easy, but God carries us through all our trials and tribulations; he doesn't necessarily take them

---

[61] https://www.merriam-webster.com/dictionary/mercy
[62] https://www.gotquestions.org/definition-of-grace.html

away. He can heal and provide for all our needs. Striving to live a Christian life is a daily journey. If you stumble, just get up and ask for forgiveness, as the Lord is forgiving, and start over. So, if I may encourage you, walking the Christian life is both fulfilling and a blessing.

Just don't give up when times get tough.

ABOUT THE AUTHOR

The writer was born and raised in Los Angeles California. She is the seventh child of eight children. Her son Ben lives in Idaho.

She obtained a bachelor's degree from Cal State Fullerton in Business Accounting.

She worked for over 40 years in banks and in a credit union. Her career began as a bank teller at the age of 17. As a loan Officer she approved and processed loans from small signature loans to corporate loans and anything in between. Her favorite type of loan was processing Real Estate Loans as she enjoyed in the excitement as people purchased their residence. She retired as the Mortgage Servicing Administrator.

In her youth the writer knew about God but her walk with God began in 1980. She was encouraged by two wonderful people. The writer began her journey as a Christian as she learns and grows in her faith constantly with God as her companion. She loves God and puts her faith and trust in Him.

www.ingramcontent.com/pod-product-compliance
Lightning Source LLC
Chambersburg PA
CBHW071342080526
44587CB00017B/2925